COLORS DEMONIC AND DIVINE

Herman Pleij

TRANSLATED BY DIANE WEBB

COLORS DEMONIC AND DIVINE

COLUMBIA UNIVERSITY PRESS   NEW YORK

Shades of Meaning in the Middle Ages and After

Columbia University Press

Publishers Since 1893

New York   Chichester, West Sussex

Translation copyright © 2004 Diane Webb

Copyright © 2002 Herman Pleij

Originally published in Dutch by Prometheus
*as Van karmijn, purper en blauw: over kleuren
van de Middeleeuwen en daarna.*

Grateful acknowledgment is made to the
Foundation for the Production and Translation
of Dutch Literature for financial support for the
translation of this work.

Library of Congress Cataloging-in-Publication Data
Pleij, Herman.
[Van karmijn, purper en blauw. English]
Colors demonic and divine : shades of meaning in the Middle
Ages and after / Herman Pleij ; translated by Diane Webb.
p. cm.
Includes bibliographical references and index.
ISBN 0–231–13022–8 (alk. paper)
1. Color—Psychological aspects—History. I. Title.

BF789.C7P5713   2004
155.9'1145'09—dc22   2003068831

∞

Columbia University Press books are printed on
permanent and durable acid-free paper.

Printed in the United States of America
Designed by Linda Secondari
c 10 9 8 7 6 5 4 3 2 1

CONTENTS

LIST OF ILLUSTRATIONS

This treatment of medieval colors and their continuing influence in our day is based on a booklet published in 1994, *Kleuren van de Middeleeuwen* (Colors of the Middle Ages), that I was asked to write for a Dutch event called "Science Week." Since then the subject has continued to haunt me and has been the source of several subsequent publications, such as the article "De onweerstaanbare opkomst van de ontkleuring" (The relentless progress of decoloration), included in my 1999 book *Tegen de barbarij* (Against barbarism). The result of my sustained interest in the subject lies before you: a greatly expanded, corrected, and up-to-date version of the original work. To my delight, a number of illustrations, which could not be included in the earlier version, have been added to the present volume.

In the past few years, acquaintances and strangers alike have supplied me with all kinds of useful information about color. In particular, the ideas of Peter Brusse, J. C. Groenewegen (of the Sikkens Foundation in Sassenheim in the Netherlands), W. P. F. van Hoogen, and Marieke van Oostrom have been a great source of inspiration for which I am especially grateful.

I strongly urge everyone to take an interest in color. Color continues to touch every facet of human existence, as it has since time immemorial. Take note of color, and you will never find yourself on a dead-end track, for there will always be interesting side paths to tempt you.

COLORS DEMONIC AND DIVINE

At last there's a new lipstick on the market that solves the embarrassing problem of smearing, always a rich source of jokes. Lipstick—the advertisement assures us—tends to rub off, but this new color, based on a scientifically tested formula, lasts for hours and hours. Should we conclude from this that certain colors are more than skin deep, that they actually penetrate below the surface?

Color has been the topic of heated debate for as long as anyone can remember. Is it an innate part of an object or a dubious additive that masks the heart of Creation? The latter, negative view of color has given rise to correspondingly negative imagery. For example, if a person gives a colored report of my words, I will probably be upset, for it means that something has been added that was not my intention, something that distorted my original meaning. This was not what Cicero had in mind in his *De Inventione* (Treatise on rhetorical invention) when he distinguished the *colores rhetorici*, a sort of verbal pigment that could be used to embellish the message so that it could be conveyed more agreeably and effectively. But what some consider a useful adornment of speech is thought by others to be a cunning attempt to hide the truth by coating it with a layer that willfully distorts its true meaning.

Any deliberate coloring of words was sheer devilry, exclaimed many people in the Middle Ages. Wasn't color a favorite ploy of Satan and his cohorts, used in their tireless efforts to trip up humanity as it struggled along the rocky path to salvation? Adherents of this theory thought color very suspect, doubly corrupted by the Fall of Man that had made the material world ephemeral and transient—and consequently a plaything of the devil. The Middle Ages also had color cultists, however, who argued that color was actually the product of a divine light that brought matter to life. Since God's very first act of creation had been to bring light into the world, it followed that colors were in the vanguard of his creative forces, even if they were elusive and intangible.

This very elusiveness has served in modern times to strengthen the idea that color is merely an accessory and not an inherent part of an object. The traditional tools of science do not permit color to be expressed as a concrete measure of space, taste, or smell. We conceive of color as a variable phenomenon of light, the perception of which can change over time. Not only that, the same person can view color differently at different times, even under seemingly identical conditions. Nowadays we prefer to think of the instability of color as a sign of its superficiality, an example—as appropriate as it is typical—of our arrogant tendency to disparage as inessential anything we cannot grasp: even in contemporary science, there are lots of sour grapes.

Everything changes. A green tree in the Middle Ages was surely not perceived in the same way as a green tree today. It differed in a variety of ways, because observers then were physically and psychologically different from observers now. To make things even more complicated, a person's perception of the "same" color is far from constant. It would even appear that colors are in our minds and by no means dependent solely on external impulses of light. You can test this hypothesis by hitting yourself in the eye and then keeping it tightly closed: you will see a star-spangled pageant exploding like fireworks against a black background. Alternatively, you can stare for a few seconds at a red square and then shift your gaze to a white surface: you will notice that the square has turned blue green. These observations are not at all the product of modern consciousness. Try looking at the sun, said Aristotle, and then close your eyes: you will see at least four colors.

Our perception of color is determined not only by such diachronic contrasts but also by the effect of simultaneous confrontation. When red is seen against a black background, it looks different from that same red seen against a white surface. But how do we know we are talking about the same red? Vincent van Gogh, color connoisseur par excellence, wrote in a letter to his brother Theo at the beginning of May 1885 that the perception of color is dependent on both the observer and the observed: "I am certain that if you were to ask Millet, Daubigny, and Corot to paint a snowy landscape without using white, they would do it, and the snow would look white in their paintings."

In the Middle Ages, the elusiveness of color was recognized not only by admirers who saw in color the divine origins of Creation but also by detractors who lamented the devil's abuse of the heavenly palette. Satan was, after all, considered capable of deluding human perception by entering the body and confounding the senses from within. What people saw as color and what proved to be so curiously inconstant was therefore an element that did not accord with divine revelation. Instead, it strove to alienate humanity from eternal truths by exchanging these truths for visual satisfaction of a very fleeting nature. Everything man saw was colored and untrue, a temptation to indulge in instant pleasures that denied eternity.

"We are blinded by colors!" Bernard of Clairvaux exclaimed repeatedly. So often in fact that in later centuries these words were regarded as his motto. This twelfth-century founder of the Cistercian order railed continually against any embellishment of earthly existence, which in his opinion was meant to unfold in the utmost simplicity. He also lashed out mercilessly at clerics who believed that God's temple should be decorated with as many treasures as possible: precious stones, paintings, brightly painted statues, and stained-glass windows: "We have gone out of the world and have left all costly and beautiful things behind for the sake of Jesus

Christ. In order to secure that same Jesus Christ, we consider to be filth everything that has an enchanting radiance, a captivating harmony, an intoxicating odor, a pleasant taste, and a delightful softness. In short, everything that tempts the body—which we strive to strengthen in devotion—is filth." In particular, Bernard considered color to be a sign of transience, an earthly veil that the devil had thrown over Creation to hide its true nature from human sight. He also thought it significant that women liked to paint themselves with bright colors in their vain quest for beauty. Hadn't women always been the devil's primary instrument of ruin, the bane of man's existence?

To promulgate this belief, medieval descriptions of the Fall of Man point to the first and cruelest color joke of all time. The apple on the tree of the knowledge of good and evil, the one Eve let the serpent tempt her into eating, had in fact displayed the most alluring colors. One side was as red as a rose, the other side was white with bits of saffron yellow. Clearly, an apple of such intriguing beauty was irresistible.

❦

Throughout the Middle Ages colors caused a great deal of commotion: the greater the outcry, the greater the apparent provocation. The debate took place at every level, even among laymen. If any one era could be singled out as being the most obsessed with color, it would be the Middle Ages.

It is important to realize that our appreciation and conceptualization of color is not fixed for all eternity. Colors, too, have a history. They are subject to a wide variety of interpretations. Even our preference for a certain color can vary considerably, depending on where we live, the era we live in, and our social standing. According to recent surveys, more than 50 percent of all the people in the Western world have a marked preference for the color blue. Green—not even a close second—is preferred by 20 percent, followed by white and red, each at around 10 percent. Yellow is one of the least favorite colors, as are brown and gray. Only in Spain is red one of the most popular colors. Children everywhere have different favorites, which proves that color preferences are culturally determined and that color is neither an intrinsic quality nor any other kind of constant.

These findings also offer insight into developments that can be clearly traced from the early Middle Ages onward. The color blue has been gaining in popularity since the twelfth century, and its rise continues unabated. Before that time, the dominant colors were not just blue but also red, white, and black. Yellow, on the other hand, has been caught in a downward spiral ever since the late Middle Ages. Fortunately, it is now one of the recognized tasks of historians to ask questions about changes in the usage, appreciation, description, and explanation of colors in the past. All this helps us to understand the attempts people made both to interpret and to subjugate their surroundings in order to attain some measure of earthly if not eternal salvation.

Colors obviously played a much more important role in the Middle Ages than they do now. This is evident first of all from the paint and color mania that swept through medieval Europe. Everything—but everything—had to be colored: food, textiles, linen, silk, leather, bone, wood, wax, illuminated manuscripts, carvings, statues, ivory, metal, human hair, beards, and even the fur and feathers of animals such as dogs, horses, and falcons. This color craze did not involve subdued colors that suited the materials in question but rather the most colorful and contrasting combinations possible. Nowadays two-toned or multicolored hair is a similar phenomenon, though such hairdos are sported only by a small (and youthful) minority.

The medieval penchant for showiness was based on ethical, aesthetic, medical, and scientific considerations. According to contemporary thought, these all came under the heading of theology, which encompassed a number of specialized fields. Everything, after all, was thought to be part of divine revelation and could be understood only within that framework. Color was thus viewed as an important part of God's grand design, which had been set down in nature. Because of their divine power of expression, specific colors could be linked to certain social classes or age groups. People used clothing to announce to the world who they were (or wanted to be) as they went about their daily lives, flaunting their feelings on the street or in the church, using their mode of dress to express what they felt about a party, a funeral, or even a proposal of marriage. The powerful language of colors—with meanings at once profound and poignant—was brought to bear on every facet of life. People wore vividly colored clothing at tournaments, of course, but also when sauntering through the streets of a town or even when attending mass, where women vied with one another for the honor of wearing the most striking colors and the latest fashions. Scarlet and crimson were especially coveted, as these costly red dyestuffs were extracted from snails and worms that were difficult to obtain.

Such color extravaganzas destabilized society because of the jealousy they provoked in the less fortunate, whose downcast state was evident from the drab, undyed clothes they wore. To their dispirited voices was added a chorus of clerics who increasingly blamed the devil for this colorful distortion of Creation. These anticolor movements presumably explain the rise in the popularity of blue, whose reflection of heavenly hues made it a very otherworldly color. Black soon joined blue as a means of expressing earthly abnegation, extreme asceticism, deep sorrow, and supreme humility. At the end of the Middle Ages, black and blue became the colors of princes and the urban aristocracy. Bright colors gradually came to represent worldly pleasures, which every civilized, God-fearing person was supposed to avoid. This is why evening dress is still black, despite—or perhaps because of—the bolder colors preferred by popular entertainers and other nouveaux riches.

These long lines run almost without interruption from the Middle Ages to the present day. Black, dark blue, and later white became noncolors, deployed to defeat the devil and his arsenal of colorful weapons. The success of the decoloration campaign can no doubt be attributed in part to Calvinism, which regarded itself as the movement's rightful heir, since decoloration was associated with the attainment of eternal life. Bright colors now belong to mass culture, sun-filled vacations, and television advertisements, with their hyped-up fears of fading caused by destructive detergents. Another sign of the times is the regimentation in sportswear, as evidenced by the sight of whole families strolling around holiday resorts and shopping malls in jogging suits of glowing purple. This was the very color that signaled distinction in the Middle Ages and was therefore the rightful property of the aristocracy.

Does this mean that this previously elite color is being democratized for the benefit of the masses? Or is it the voice of advertising that we hear, calling for a sporty return to nature by way of gleaming pastels, which in turn might spark off a revival of the kaleidoscopic colors of the Middle Ages? Since we dare not go straight back to medieval times, we apparently need the intermediate step of in-between shades. This is obvious from the ubiquitous pastel shades of bathrooms, bed linen, lingerie, and nightclothes.

Is there no going back to the bright hues and bold contrasts of the Middle Ages? The masses would never instigate such a movement, though they might jump on the bandwagon once it got rolling. The modern elite continues to shun bright colors as they become increasingly estranged from nature. These days we experience color chiefly through artificial means: bigger and better television screens, movies, glossy magazines, and such unnatural permutations as genetically engineered tulips and metallically shining automobiles. We go out of our way to behold both the tender green of spring and the spectacular shades of autumn. There are even organized tours—the foliage tours in New England, for example—that bring us closer to nature and allow us to experience it first-hand. When we do, nature can come as a pleasant surprise—in the spring, say, when we catch our first glimpse of bright yellow fields of mustard surrounded by luscious green meadows. In the Middle Ages, though, people were constantly surrounded by the colors of nature. That in itself was enough to make them seek a deeper meaning in colors. Nature's palette spoke for itself. Until relatively recently, however, the world has been reproduced for us mainly in black and white, through woodcuts, engravings, newspapers, photographs, films, and television. Even now, though we take great pains to reproduce natural hues as faithfully as possible, the technical means of color reproduction at our disposal are still fairly new, and the results are unreliable and relatively expensive. The bewildering differences in color reproductions of famous paintings, for example, can be quite startling. Even so, once color entered the arena of mass communication, it was here to stay, despite the fact that newspapers and press photographs are still largely black and white.

On the whole, the recent color boom has lent black and white a new dignity. Less is more, as far as color and fashion are concerned. Art films are produced in black and white, as are most of the photographs exhibited in galleries and museums. Elegant automobiles are either black or gray. Postmodern bars and restaurants in fashionable city centers tend to be decorated in black and white. Movements like those of the 1960s, which sought to revive the riotous colors of the Middle Ages, prove to have been brief outbursts that confirmed rather than denied the hegemony of black and blue. In any case, for centuries, a strong undercurrent of anticolor sentiment has been leading us further and further away from color.

There are many facets involved in the study of color. Developments in the methods of describing, interpreting, appreciating, creating, and using colors make them a handy gauge of human civilization. In the Middle Ages, people were truly obsessed with color, but was it an instrument of the devil or an ornament of God? This book will attempt to elucidate the use to which color was put in medieval times and the effect it has had on modern society. After all, we are the heirs of the past, and that includes the colors of the Middle Ages.

CHAPTER ONE

Medieval Notions of Color

Color cannot be assigned a dimension, size, or number. If we wish to say something about color, therefore, we must rely on impressions formed under varying temporal and spatial conditions affecting both the observer and the observed. Modern color reproductions would seem to facilitate communication on the subject, but the problem remains the same: the perception of color is based on personal impressions of a rather haphazard nature.

A pamphlet from 1542—chosen at random from the many precursors of the newspaper published in Antwerp at this time—contains a sensational report of a plague of grasshopperlike creatures that were afflicting Italy. These insects, though, were much more terrifying than grasshoppers, because they were purported to be an instrument of God's wrath. They were monstrous in every sense and "of a color similar to goose dung." To describe a color with the greatest possible accuracy, the author chose a frame of reference that reflected the general knowledge and realm of experience of his readers, who certainly knew what goose droppings looked like. Nowadays we would probably have to look it up, unless we happen to be farmers, biologists, or bird-watchers. In any case, "goose-turd green" is doubtless a different hue now than it was then. Clearly, we will never be able to ascertain the true color of those insects.

Color is not a substance but a quality made manifest by light. It is based on our perception of the light reflected by an object. This concept has been generally accepted only since the seventeenth century, when Newton used a prism to refract a ray of white light into its component colors, producing chromatic dispersion. Without light there is no color. The color of an object is determined by two factors: the type of light and its intensity. The sensitivity of an illuminated surface to the different components of light also plays a role. If an object reflects the red in a light ray but absorbs the other components, we perceive that object as red. Color thus depends on the capacity of a surface, whether painted or not, to absorb light of various intensities.

In the Middle Ages, color was generally seen as a substance that was created or rendered visible by light refracting from an object. Sometimes, color seems to have been thought of simply as light changed into matter. According to Thomas Aquinas, light collided with objects of varying transparency and permeability. This caused the light to diffract and take on the hue potentially present in the object, which only light could bring out and make visible. From this line of reasoning it followed that objects of clarity and brilliance gave rise to the most beautiful colors.

While Aristotle (referred to in the Middle Ages simply as "The Philosopher") believed that color was primarily a quality inherent in objects, in the thirteenth century the learned encyclopedist Vincent of Beauvais expanded the notion of color by suggesting the existence of duality: color is an inherent part of things but also part of the light illuminating them. To illustrate the dual nature of color, he took white as an example. White is the color of snow and therefore the result of cold, whereas the white in quicklime and plaster is clearly the result of heat. This can only be explained if another factor comes into play, and this factor must be light.

Color, at any rate, was closely connected with the bearer of it— whether a bodily characteristic or an inanimate object—which implied that color said something significant about the very essence of a person or thing. In the Middle Ages, therefore, an object and its color were thought to be vitally connected. Not only could this connection be revealed, it could also be applied at will by adding layers of color—and therefore layers of meaning—to an object. In many languages, the words "color" and "paint" stem from the words for "cover" and "skin." In Latin, for example, "*color*" is derived from "*celare*" or "*occulere*," to cover up. This notion misled theologians like Bernard of Clairvaux into thinking that color was a worldly gloss and therefore unnecessary or even dangerous, because the devil tended to use such earthly elements to bait his traps. Moreover, this color cover-up concealed the true nature of things. In Middle Dutch, the word "*colour*" could also be used to mean "gloss."

Nevertheless, among scholars, the positive connotations of the word gained the upper hand. Their definitions generally began with etymologies, for even the spectrum of words used to refer to colors could not be fortuitous. The instigator of this method was Isidore of Seville, a theologian and archbishop who at the beginning of the seventh century compiled an immense encyclopedia, based on word derivations, in which he attempted to explain the whole of Creation. He linked the word "color" to "*calor*," heat, with the following explanation: "Colors are so called because the heat of a fire or the sun gives rise to them."

Medieval scholars constantly linked colors with brilliance, intensity, and luminosity. This explains their many references to precious stones, which caused light to burst into the most exciting colors. The scholarly elite agreed that colors exerted a powerful influence, and they were not alone in this conviction. It was also prevalent in popular culture, so often a breeding ground for *exempla*, the exemplary stories used to spice up lay sermons. The following story serves to illustrate this point: A heavily pregnant woman lay tossing and turning in bed, dwelling on the blackamoor's head on the signboard across the street. All day long she lay there staring, unable to take her eyes off it. Shortly thereafter she gave birth to a black baby, much to her husband's consternation. The couple concluded that the sign must have been to blame. Woe betide those who underestimate the power of color!

Similar tall tales were even told by the enlightened Karel van Mander, a Renaissance literary man and painter obsessed with classicist ideals. Van Mander's education did not prevent him from dredging up old superstitions about color in his 1604 treatise *Den grondt der edel vry schilder-const* (Foundation of the noble, liberal art of painting). He, too, tells stories of women giving birth to babies who were the color their mothers had been thinking of at conception or who displayed blemishes of a hue that had frightened the mother when pregnant. If she had been particularly afraid of bleeding, for example, her children would be born with red birthmarks.

Seen from this very medieval viewpoint, color is a dangerous disease that threatens to attack the core of every creature's being. Van Mander emphasized the perils of surface contamination by repeating the old wives' tale that fruit or flower stains on a baby's face would leave lasting blemishes if they were not wiped off immediately. Perhaps he intended these bizarre anecdotes as reminders of the familiar dualistic thinking of the Middle Ages, in which things were either good or evil, heavenly or earthly, divine or diabolical. This also explains why color had to have a negative side.

Van Mander's opening exposition on the essence of color, however, testifies to considerably more balanced thinking. He begins by declaring that colors are inherent in the created world: the divine act of creation endowed all things not only with life but also with specific colors.

The *Blason des couleurs* (Blazon of colors)—a heraldic treatise published in the mid-fifteenth century—gives much simpler examples to demonstrate the power of color. Even ponderous elephants can be spurred to action by color. At the sight of red or green, they will readily attack anything that crosses their path, and, according to medieval notions, this is exactly what they were meant to do: the Bible, after all, assures us that beasts were supposed to be subservient to humans in every respect. All one had to do was to discover in the case of each animal how this divine plan could best be realized. Incidentally, this text, written by Jehan Courtois, also known as Sicily Herald, was the most important source for Karel van Mander, whose notions of color were firmly rooted in the Middle Ages.

❀

The connection of color with light and brilliance suggests a direct link with divine revelation, often depicted as a ray of light illuminating the earth. Presumably this is why the power of color was held to be so great. Colors contributed to the revelation of the divine mystery. The trick was to interpret them properly.

Light and color are at their finest and most revealing when they join forces in the stained-glass windows of churches and cathedrals. The light striking the painted glass causes the colors to explode and spill forth into the church. Many contemporaries described their first sight of light breaking through stained-glass windows as the ultimate in beauty. "What is more beautiful than light," said Hugo of St. Victor, "which, itself colorless, nonetheless brings out clearly the color of all things?" The architectural plans of Gothic cathedrals were aimed primarily at imposing structure on light and color, demonstrating above all else how God—coming from the east—took possession every morning of his bride, the Church.

In fact, all churches were supposed to be copies of the heavenly Jerusalem. According to the description in the Book of Revelation (chapters 21 and 22), the eternal city was constructed completely of gold, silver, and precious stones. Absolute and definitive brilliance was thus formalized in a way that consigned all temporalities to oblivion. Clearly, the actual decoration of the churches on earth could not hope to compete with their celestial counterpart, no matter how many precious objects were stuffed into their interiors. Still, special effects could be achieved by projecting the heavenly Jerusalem onto those cold, gray walls in the form of sparkling colors that burst into the church through its stained-glass windows:

heavenly architecture, carried out by earthly architects—often the abbot, prior, or bishop himself.

Most medieval scholars saw colors as vital messengers, cornerstones of the complicated order that governs and guides Creation. This resulted in an unseemly scramble to assign meanings to the various colors and to reveal their connection with the other elements of Creation. The whole process hinged on what were sometimes radically different standpoints, which—just to complicate matters—were continually being replaced by new points of view. There is no such thing as an unequivocal system of medieval color symbolism, unless the term is used to refer to medieval man's desperate and contradictory attempts to cast colors in the role of meaningful signs planted along the narrow path to eternal salvation.

Time and again, however, these efforts—which appear confused to us nowadays—represented the search for a God-given order, which sinful and flawed humanity had found so difficult to decipher since the Fall. The devil was always standing by, ready to confound our powers of perception, forcing us to focus on a wide range of earthly temptations. Humankind was bent not so much on understanding that lost order as on restoring it. In the Middle Ages, comprehension and explanation primarily meant establishing order or, rather, reestablishing the order lost when the Fall threw everything into such painful disarray.

Everything had to be arranged according to the original plan and linked to the other elements of Creation. The human race was constantly striving to regain its ability to discover the order it had so foolishly forfeited. Reaching the New Jerusalem by negotiating this earthly maze would restore contact with that order. The only hope of getting there, however, was learning to read the signs along the way. All the unbridled, intellectual juggling with Creation harked back to this unshakable belief. Everything had to be explained and put in its proper place. Only then would it be possible for us to climb out of the vale of tears into which the devil had cast us.

Everything, therefore, was linked to everything else, which is why colors were assigned to the four elements, the four seasons, the four points of the compass, the four temperaments, the stages of human life, the seven planets, the periods of sacred history, precious stones, feast days, ecclesiastical vestments, and much, much more. The technique used to determine the place and meaning of a certain color within this order entailed the establishment of simple associations, usually based on presumed word derivations.

Surely this was what God had intended when he gave us color. The title of a fourteenth-century Dutch verse leaves us in no doubt: "On six colors and the twelve-year stages of life, the one explained by the other":

Six colors our God did bestow
On his Creation here below,
In his munificence and grace,
So with free will the human race
Could know their God and thereby learn
To thank and worship him in turn.

The author then connects white-silver (referring to the color by both its common name and its heraldic tincture, *argent*) with the first twelve-year stage of human life, when the child is pure and untainted—in fact angelic. Green-vermilion stands for the age of youth between twelve and twenty-four, a period of growth comparable to spring, a season bursting with energy. The stages continue until the black-sable stage between sixty and seventy-two, expressive of simplicity and acquiescence.

The colors noted in the Bible were obviously a good place to start, although there are fewer references to them than one would imagine. Mention is usually made of the colors of the horses in the Book of Revelation (6:2–8): white, red, black, and buff-colored (described as "pale" in the King James version). The various colors of the curtains in the tabernacle in Exodus (26:1)—blue, purple, and scarlet—determined the choice of liturgical colors as officially decreed by Pope Innocent III (d. 1216). He also assigned four main colors to the various feast days: white for Christmas, Easter, Ascension, and the other feasts honoring God and the Holy Family; red for Pentecost, the feasts of the Holy Cross, and the feast days of the martyrs; green for the Sundays after Epiphany, the Trinity, and all working days; black for Advent, Lent, Good Friday, and All Souls' Day. Moreover, the earth was linked to the color white, the sea to purple, the heavens to hyacinth blue, and fire to crimson. To these same colors Thomas Aquinas then assigned virtues and moral values, purity being white, martyrdom purple, a yearning for immortality blue, and love red.

These were the foundations on which mankind continued endlessly to build. It was not a very concerted effort, because many a medieval scholar introduced a rival model or added a floor to the building that threatened to make the whole structure come tumbling down. But each new attempt testified to a deep desire to decipher the signs that God had incidentally—some thought expressly—provided in color.

Despite all these differences in interpretation, the tone was set by a color scheme dominated by white, red, and black—the colors of the horses in the Book of Revelation—sometimes joined by green or yellowish green. This notion persisted until the end of the Middle Ages, as did the rather fixed associations of these colors with the gifts of the Holy Spirit: piety, fortitude, charity, and hope. Anyone who did not know enough to wear these colors was obviously mad. In a late-medieval song, fools proudly declare their aversion to green, white, black, and red: where was greater idiocy to be found?

> We're crazy sots, it is our lot;
> To this we are not blind!
> In this world of sin, we make a din,
> We've clearly lost our mind.
> We know not green, white, black, or red;
> Have you seen greater fools of late?
> Our lunacy is so widespread,
> We'll be quite mad until we're dead;
> For spouting nonsense is our fate!

These colors, it was generally believed, had shaped the world, and they still reigned supreme. The great Flemish poet Jacob van Maerlant, for example, reported that these were the colors that had decorated the walls of Troy. And the German author Walther von der Vogelweide maintained that these four colors held sway over the whole of Creation: "On the outside the world is beautifully white, green, and red, and on the inside black and somber as death."

Red-white-black became the basic color scheme, a development that is more logical than it might seem at first glance. For centuries, red—not black—was thought to be the exact opposite of white. The devil, for example, was often portrayed in red. In tales of chivalry such as *Walewein*, red-clad knights are cast in a negative role. Even more revealing is the fact that until well into the twelfth century such intellectual games as chess and checkers were played with red and white pieces. Gradually, however, darker hues began to make headway. The devil was portrayed with increasing frequency in black, and red knights were pushed to the sidelines by black knights. In the knightly epic *Karel ende Elegast*, Elegast chooses black armor when he is forced to conceal his identity. When his blamelessness emerges at the end of the story, however, he immediately sheds his black exterior.

The persistence of this color scheme can also be explained by its mythical underpinnings. In the fairy tale "Little Red Riding Hood," a girl dressed in red brings white butter to a supposed grandmother decked out in black. In "Snow White," a witch dressed in black brings a red apple to a girl whose complexion is whiter than white. The same mythical values return in Hitler's swastika symbolism, which made use of these three ur-colors.

Blue and related hues did not begin to come into their own until the thirteenth century (see figs. 1, 2, and 3). Their rise in popularity, however, did not cause the red-white-black color scheme to fall from its pedestal; instead, the color blue took its place alongside these hues as their worthy companion. Blue's acceptance was hastened when aristocrats began to favor blue as the most suitable color for high-quality fabrics. In fact, the color blue took the world by storm, with a swiftness that had serious economic repercussions for the producers of dyestuffs.

In the Rhine valley, the dealers in madder reacted in a remarkable way. The madder plant was the source of a red pigment used in dyeing clothes, but the madder trade was seriously threatened by the sudden demand for blue dyes. In response, the madder merchants petitioned the painters working on Strasbourg Cathedral to portray the devils on the walls and stained-glass windows in blue, so as to discredit the color.

It was at this time, too, that people began to acquire a taste for mixed colors and in-between shades, which could strengthen the effect of the primary colors and show them to the best advantage. At the same time, scholars were engaged in a heated dispute about which colors were primary and which only secondary. Their learned opinions were often based on interpretations of the colors of the rainbow that dated from classical antiquity and the early Middle Ages.

From all this theorizing, there emerged not only an endless number of definitions and classifications but also a staggering number of recipes for dyestuffs. Pigments were extracted from animals, plants, and minerals. Not only were there vast differences in quality, but the makeup of any given pigment was also determined by the nature of the object to be dyed or painted. Exclusivity was sought not only in the rarity of the ingredients but also in the ingenuity of the recipes themselves.

The urban dyeing industry was therefore shrouded in great secrecy. Occultism and other forms of magic played an important role, especially in attempts to discredit competitors. The tales surrounding the supposed invention of oil paint by Jan van Eyck are a good example and also serve to explain how the cloth dyers managed to form such powerful guilds in the cities. The success of the dye merchants' efforts to demonize their rivals, however, led to dyers in general being accused of engaging in illicit practices, poisoning the air, polluting the water, and even conspiring with the devil.

Such accusations must be seen in the wider context of much older allegations that dyers were meddling with God's Creation by falsifying its true colors. Ever since the early days of Christianity, deliberate attempts to turn one substance into another had been frowned on in orthodox circles. Dyers were often thought of as swindlers, for they could use their brightly colored dyes to breathe new life into any old cast-off, naturally with a view to huge profits. Apparently their dubious practices were so widespread that such artifice could be advertised with impunity in books containing instructions for the mixing and application of paint. The popular *Batement van recepten* (Spectacle of recipes), printed in Antwerp in 1549, blithely offers professional copyists a recipe enabling them "to write or calligraph gold letters that look just like gold without really being gold." Horse traders, furthermore, are given a recipe "to color or dye the mane and tail of a horse at their own discretion." From the recipe, it emerges that the color in question is black—naturally, because the horse would then look younger and sprightlier and doubtless fetch a higher price.

It is hardly surprising, then, that in contemporary literature dyers come off badly in comparison with other artisans. A humorous French-Dutch schoolbook used in mid-fourteenth-century Bruges places the working classes of the city in a neutral or positive light, which makes the negative attitude to the cloth dyers all the more apparent: "Elias, the dyer, has recently moved from the place where he used to live. He takes far too long to dye my cloth, and I will undoubtedly have to pay too much for it." Elias dawdled because he charged by the hour. That his contemporaries found his behavior suspect is evident from the fact that he is introduced as a person who has just moved house. A trustworthy citizen had a fixed abode, and, if he abandoned it, it was a sign that he felt the need to hotfoot it to safety. A later version of this schoolbook, dating from 1501, added that Elias used inferior dyes, which meant that his cloth would fade quickly.

In class satire, a popular literary genre in those days, similar attacks on dyers and painters form a proper subgenre. Around 1562, in Haarlem, a black comedy was performed in which the devil-in-chief—Lucifer—extols cloth dyers as the best-loved inhabitants of his diabolical domain: "The cloth dyers daily go about their cunning business. They habitually hang their cloth in the smoke, to make it look more blue. And if I were to reveal all I know about their mischievous malpractices, I would surely put these impostors to shame." Elsewhere in the play, Lucifer also introduces painters, glassblowers, and sculptors as kindred crooks "who mislead folk with their bizarre transformations."

The catalyst that triggered this literary offensive was, quite simply, the reality of the situation. In 1554 the Haarlem dyers' guild began requiring new members to take an oath, swearing to refrain from fraudulent practices such as applying a bogus black made from inferior pigments or using other substandard materials specified in the oath. And in Leiden, the textile center par excellence, attempts were made from the late Middle Ages onward to combat the artifice and sleight of hand practiced by the cloth dyers, which rose to alarming heights during the sixteenth century, especially among the blue dyers, who represented the most lucrative sector. To dye is to deceive. And appearances are deceptive, even in their most elementary form.

❀

In reality, the brightly colored Middle Ages are only half the story. Or perhaps a quarter of it. Nowadays we prefer to see those times as a gaudy world in which life was lived as it was meant to be, as a permanent celebration of the senses. But a lot was uncolored in the Middle Ages and remained so, sometimes by choice but more often because dyes were so expensive. Colors emphasized wealth and were therefore used to express power, ostentation, consequence, and distinction. Both the higher clergy and the nobility exploited these uses, while at the same time claiming to distance themselves from the overpowering language of color.

Peasants, workers, and the lower middle classes, however, simply couldn't afford brilliant or even lasting colors. Shirts, doublets, stockings, and kerchiefs were often treated with vegetable dyes, with such inadequate results that a shower of rain would wash out the color in the peasants' blue smocks. Unlike the picture painted by many films, medieval villages and cities were inconceivably gray and dismal, even more than we imagine a nineteenth-century manufacturing town to have been. As a result, a nobleman riding past in his scarlet or purple cloak would have stood out all the more.

The wildest stories were told about the manufacture of the costliest dyes. Dyers were likened to alchemists, conjuring and experimenting with secret recipes. Purple pigment came from rare snails and also—according to Jacob van Maerlant—from the blood of elephants. He also claimed that the most exclusive red was obtained from a small mussel-like fish found in the Baltic Sea. Extracting it was a laborious process, because the artery containing the precious substance could only be reached by drilling a hole in a live fish. If the fish died during the operation, it would immediately spew out all the color, which could no longer be recovered. Plainly, such colors were meant to be worn only by those of the highest orders.

In any event, color in the Middle Ages resided mainly in the cities. It was there that the noble households, religious processions, and numerous festivals colorfully proclaimed their importance and defined their attitudes. It was there, too, that people bound themselves by the color of their clothes to the classes to which they belonged, by birth, choice, or necessity. Colors were still a long way from being democratized.

CHAPTER TWO

Color in Daily Life

Color could also be a weapon. The heart of many a writer and chronicler leapt at the sight of the banners, flags, and blazons of battling knights whose bright, contrasting colors were meant to radiate self-confidence and invite challenge. Writing around 1190, the troubadour Bertran de Born could hardly contain himself when contemplating a scene of battle: "I love to see the meadows full of tents and flags. Verily, eating, drinking, and sleeping are less enjoyable than hearing the cry of 'Charge!' when the horses are standing under the trees, whinnying in expectation." The combatants themselves also thought of their glorious past in terms of provocative colors. A knight who took part in the first crusade of 1095–96, for example, remembered "shields shining with precious stones and painted in a dazzling array of colors."

Knightly tales and epic poems also describe great excitement at the prospect of the coming battle, marked by the ensigns of war, the colors that each side planted in the enemy's sight. In the romance *Walewein*, the lord of a castle is startled when he wakes up to find a vast army encamped before his walls: "He went to the window and looked outside, at the green grass. But no matter where he looked, in every direction he saw pitched tents—green, blue, yellow, and red—and on many tents a large eagle of brightly shining gold. God, how many fine swords there were, as well as helmets, spears, and pennants in shades of yellow, gray, red, and green!"

War was waged with visors open, as free men facing one another, a notion so deeply ingrained in the etiquette of battle that five centuries later, at the beginning of the First World War, French soldiers left the trenches and ran across open fields in bright red trousers to attack enemy lines. They were mowed down in their thousands by machine guns.

The fourteenth-century French chronicler Froissart always flew into joyful raptures when treated to the sight of warships with flags and pennants flying, their colorful coats of arms glittering in the sun. And he was equally overcome with joy to see the sun playing on the helmets, suits of armor, lance tips, pennons, and banners of horsemen engaged in a cavalry march.

Colors could be put to use just as aggressively in sacred texts. In the fourteenth century, the great mystic Jan van Ruusbroec launched an attack on the indifferent masses who ignored the sacrifice Christ had made for them on the cross. He described the Savior's bleeding wounds and the colorful cloak in which he was wrapped: "He was then so scourged and beaten that his body was emptied of its precious blood. After that he was given a cloak the color of purple, the blood-red made from the blood of fish. And it was lined with fiery scarlet extracted from the blood of worms." The same words are repeated, almost exactly, later in the text. Continual exposure to similar texts in sermons and other discourse made it difficult to experience the color red in any other dimension. Red is the color of blood. And blood is first and foremost the blood of Christ, which was shed for us. Anyone who might have forgotten that fact was reminded of it by the countless texts appearing after Ruusbroec, which used similarly aggressive terms in an attempt to rouse people from their lethargy and move them to compassion.

Clothing did indeed have an amazing ability to radiate power. Quality, rareness, and color all determined its capacity for expression, which in the course of the Middle Ages became increasingly subject to rules and especially to prohibitions. Clothing reflected social standing, sex, age, civil status, and occupation. Only country folk and members of the lower middle class were excluded from this colorful rivalry. Their drab, undyed garments could not possibly compete with the dazzling dress donned by the bourgeoisie, the nobility, and the higher clergy. Not only do the colorful Middle Ages contrast with the tonally much flatter present, but within the Middle Ages there was a veritable clash of palettes among the various classes.

Such excesses regularly spun out of control. A Flemish chronicle of 1531 blames the war between Ghent and Bruges that took place in 1379 primarily on the arrogance that drove the masses to the height of folly. Their vanity manifested itself in ostentatious dress and outclassed the nobility in extravagance: "Even simple folk were wearing two-toned trousers and shoes with long, pointed toes, silver belts weighing a couple of pounds, cloaks down to their ankles, expensively lined with fine cloth, caps and overgarments, decoratively trimmed at the hem, and hats fit for princes or nobles." In the countryside, too, women working as laborers, milkmaids, fishwives, and vegetable sellers wore several layers of clothing and costly veils, "lined at the front with red silk or green velvet." And on holidays they made so bold as to wear "scarlet caps with enameled silver buttons."

The court was crawling with colors. Knights brandishing banners, diplomats identifiable by their coats of arms, messengers in livery, purveyors wearing the colors of their guilds—they all wore striking hues designed to identify themselves and to announce their presence loudly. On public and religious holidays and at tournaments and other festivities, one could feast one's eyes on such a wealth of color that it was all a herald could do to identify and interpret the signs and marshal the participants accordingly.

This explosion of color at court was so widespread and imbued with meaning that it became not only the hallmark of courtly and knightly life, tournament, and battle but also an important part of the perception of color as such. It is no coincidence that in the French version of the *Roman de la Rose* (*The Romance of the Rose*) the personification of Art attempts to immortalize such events.

The author concludes ironically that Art never progresses beyond imitation (including exaggeration) and can never really bring anything to life:

> Art paints and forges, cuts and colors
> Knights, battle-ready, in full armor
> On their chargers, wildly keen
> Their coats of arms blue, yellow, green
> Or other hues upon their shield
> If you would still more colors wield.

Heralds—the professional experts on heraldic colors and signs at the courts of Europe—strove to record their knowledge in reference works, attempting to describe the coats of arms of the entire European nobility as well as to reveal the underlying meanings of these identification badges. Sicily Herald, who served at the court of King René of Anjou, spoke in compelling terms about the language of color in his *Blason des couleurs* (Blazon of colors). This extremely popular work, dating from the mid-fifteenth century (and perhaps expanded by an anonymous successor), was reprinted until well into the sixteenth century.

It did not meet with everyone's approval, however. Rabelais, an enlightened humanist, thought this text represented everything that was reprehensible about the Middle Ages. He was especially critical of the author's tendency to assign a moral and theological meaning to every natural phenomenon. Rabelais used his novel *Gargantua and Pantagruel* to launch his criticism, devoting no less than two chapters to color symbolism.

Rabelais's hero had a heraldic device in white and blue, colors indicative of celestial joy. To the hero's father, "white meant joy, pleasure, delight, and rejoicing, and blue meant heavenly things." Rabelais then addressed the reader: "You'll say that white means faith and blue means steadfastness and determination." And who had put such ideas into his readers' heads? "A beaten-up old book, sold by door-to-door peddlers" (a sly dig at the old aristocracy, who looked on this exclusive little volume as something of a gospel). Rabelais then condemned the book's contents as well as the author's insolence in thinking he could dictate the meaning of color. Those who heeded such rubbish were "doddering old idiots" who had actually "harnessed their mules, dressed their pages, designed their breeches, embroidered their gloves, fringed their bed curtains, painted their banners and flags, composed their songs, and (this is the worst of it) created deception and all manner of deviltry . . . for who knows what evil messages can be sent by wearing the wrong colors?"

Just how serious Rabelais took the matter emerges in another chapter, in which he discloses how color symbolism should be put to use, his exposition being based on the colors white and blue. According to Rabelais, explications of the meaning of color in nature should be based on both philosophical reasoning and ancient authority. It is also essential that everyone endorse such argumentation unhesitatingly, since the meaning of color is self-evident. Rabelais had nothing against color symbolism; he simply disapproved of medieval methodology. Oddly enough, many of his proposals accord with that methodology, while much of what he reproached Sicily Herald for cannot be found in the latter's work. Rabelais may have been confusing him with someone else, whose work had been printed anonymously.

Sicily Herald's *Blason des couleurs*, against which Rabelais raged so fiercely, marks the end of a development. In plain and practical language, the author explains to a courtly public which colors are to be worn by representatives of the various classes, age groups, and occupations and on which occasions. He goes on to summarize the results of ten centuries of scholarship—a frequent source of academic strife. From this wealth of material, Sicily Herald makes his choice, often without giving his reasons, for he is utterly lacking in scholarly pretensions.

Sicily Herald aimed at nothing more than to produce a handy little reference book for everyday use. It is possible that the book was commissioned by his patron, René of Anjou, as this is just the kind of work heralds were employed to do. In any case, it was intended for people who were frequently in the public eye, such as official representatives and envoys. Yet everyone could benefit from reading this book, which explains why Sicily Herald wrote it in the vernacular.

❀

It was initially a courtly public that avidly sought information and instruction on which colors to wear. New models of aristocratic behavior were emerging, which were put to the test mainly in play-acting and recitation. It is to these developments that we owe a literature rich in love lyrics, knightly epics, and moralizing allegories.

These verses and plays demonstrated the new models of behavior by giving examples—derived from both classical antiquity and contemporary sources—which sometimes took the form of debates or riddles but also found expression in explicit narratives and songs. Such texts were sung, recited, acted out, or listened to by the whole court. Whether or not they were led by a professional entertainer, these performances often required the ladies to play important roles. Active participation at all levels meant that these works caught on quickly, and the nouveaux riches in the cities soon followed suit. It is hardly surprising, then, that publishers continued to print and distribute texts like these until well into the sixteenth century.

Such playacting—expressed in verse or more elaborate dramatic forms—sometimes focused on the color and meaning of the clothes worn by lovers, about which there was a strong consensus of opinion. There was, however, disagreement about whether it was desirable for lovers to make a public display of their feelings and moods by wearing clothes that sent signals for all to see.

The most innocent texts are the ones that try to explain the meaning of vivid colors in clothing. The virtues are personified as women, whose characters are expressed by the color of their dress. Fidelity wears black, Honor gold, Chastity white, Constancy blue,

Love red, and Protection green. These colors occur in such a large number of combinations that all the colors and virtues appear to be interchangeable. Elsewhere, in the work of the Dutch poet Dirc Potter, Dame Temperance wears the green cloak of hope, Wisdom the white cloak of immaculateness, Strength the red cloak of joy, and Justice the blue cloak of unwavering faith.

Eustache Deschamps, a poet at the French court, introduced a piquant note by having lovers air their feelings in the colors of their clothing. One of his poems describes lovers dressing in various colors for their mistresses. The one who cloaks himself in black is indeed a pitiable wretch: though desiring his beloved the most, he is crippled by the sorrow of rejection.

> One dons the color green for her,
> Another white, another blue,
> Another still a blood-red hue,
> And he who is the most lovelorn
> Must dress in black and, lovesick, mourn.

This tradition apparently arose in German-speaking regions, where the beginnings of such playacting were seen in the thirteenth century. These practices were then fashionably followed by the Dutch, who picked up a lot of courtly ritual from the Germans and translated it into a German-tinged literary language of their own.

Colors were thus capable of revealing the stage of passion in which a lover found or imagined himself. Green expressed hope, white indicated faith in a happy outcome, blue implied steadfastness, brown suggested appropriate humility and modesty, yellow-gold meant the fulfillment of love, gray indicated servitude, and black was a sign of mourning for a lost love. Here, too, there were many alternative meanings, just as there were always disagreements about the interpretation of signs in nature. The subject even inspired the writing of plays in which actors took the parts of colors, who then quarreled with a lady or one another about their own meaning and value. A funny situation arose when a woman was asked to judge a motley company of lovers, parading before her in all shapes and sizes, each trying to outdo the others in declaiming his ambitions and frustrations.

This could lead to harsh rejections, as in the *Spiel von den sieben Farben* (Play of the seven colors), dating from the fifteenth century. The female protagonist is offended by the practice of wearing red clothes to advertise passion: after all, many people dress in red without giving a thought to love. She is irritated by the foolishness that prompts a young man to wear white because he is filled with hope. Such sentiments must never be put on display; hope in such matters should be nurtured in secret. Publicly parading high hopes of love will only elicit ridicule. Her temper really flares, though, when a lover presents himself in yellow, a sign that his ultimate wish has been granted by his beloved and his suffering is over. Scandalous, the woman exclaims. When your beloved has given herself to you, you must never betray it by your mode of dress. You should keep such intimacies to yourself. This applies in general to the color coding of clothes worn during courtship. Some things are better left unsaid, but if a man and woman really feel the need to demonstrate their private feelings, then both would do best to dress in brown, which signifies complete and utter devotion.

Shortly before this, the candid Christine de Pisan had already spoken out against the superficial language of love as voiced by the color of clothing. Dressing in blue as a declaration of faithfulness in love was beside the point; the important thing was true dedication and protection. Besides, she added, perhaps this very blue was being worn to conceal the truth:

> Wearing blue does not win my support,
> Not in blazonry, nor love of woman,
> But faithfully to serve with a sound heart
> Her, above all, keep from defamation
> Love doth burgeon, not in wearing blue
> But some people indeed put on that hue
> Thus hiding several evil deeds from view
> Deceiving easily by wearing blue . . .

For Christine, the language of color masked the falseness and deceit that could lurk behind a seemingly innocent exterior.

How serious was such courtly playacting? Did one actually wear certain colors to express emotions? On the whole, it is not easy to determine the extent to which all this show of color actually translated into a new code of courtesy among nobles, merchants, magistrates, and their wives. To begin with, there were the clear signals given by a knight at his investiture. The white robe stood for his cleanliness of body, while the scarlet cloak recalled his paramount duty of shedding blood in the defense of the Church. Brown stockings were meant to remind him of the earth to which he would return, and the display of humility this required was accentuated by the white girdle of chastity. This was, however, no more than a ritual gesture, the expression of an ideal that was apparently satisfied—as was so much medieval allegory and symbolism—to remain an idea or at most a game: we encounter very few knights actually wearing this hallowed costume.

Nevertheless, it is not unlikely that clothing was in fact allowed to speak a language of its own. A great deal of evidence has been collected showing that a more refined sort of behavior, based on aloofness and subtle signals, became the prescribed way to distinguish oneself from the masses. The habits described and illustrated in etiquette books, tales of chivalry, and love songs thoroughly insinuated themselves into the daily routine of the elite and those aspiring to such circles.

René of Anjou, king of Sicily in the mid-fifteenth century, manipulated his whole court by parading his feelings in front of them, as though he felt compelled to dramatize all those courtly plays and poems in his daily life. The state of his emotions was immediately apparent from the livery of his court attendants: whenever his hopes had been dashed, for example, they were clad in a combination of black, white, and gray. All-black attire could be interpreted in a number of ways, though none of its meanings strayed far from the realm of solemnity, sorrow, or joy at the prospect of the afterlife. Dark gray indicated high hopes, but then the pages would suddenly be instructed to don violet or white—as a token of the king's faithfulness in love—only to be told a short time later to change into black or dark red when their master, indignant and mournful, had decided to turn his back on the world.

⚘

Townspeople developed a deep distrust of the assertiveness radiated by colorful clothing. Color became the lingua franca for inter-class communication, strongly emphasizing the growing contrasts between the various urban milieus. This emphasis was needless, according to some, who were increasingly successful in forcing civic authorities to impose restrictions that quickly turned into full-fledged prohibitions.

The debate about the acceptability of certain colors had started long before this. The desire to distance oneself from color had been clearly demonstrated by the Franciscans, who had decided to wear gray habits instead of the black of the Benedictines or the white of the Cistercians. In their eyes, black and white—expressing humility and heavenly joy, respectively—were colors, pure and simple, and as such liable to contamination by the devil. The Franciscans had therefore resolved to wear habits made of undyed cloth, which could be gray, ashen, or brown, depending on the nature of the fabric. Their fundamental precept of mendicancy thus found expression in their rejection of colors, which were, after all, prime examples of the frivolous embellishment of earthly materiality. And wasn't it evident from the scant and stereotyped attention it received in the Bible that color was in fact unimportant?

Clerical debate focused on the question of whether one should praise God in terms of total plainness or dazzling brilliance, using the tools he himself had bestowed upon Creation: the white, black, and brown of monks as opposed to the lilac, purple, and scarlet of bishops and cardinals. The nobility entered the ecclesiastical fray with alacrity, steering the discussion in the direction of the three estates and the necessity of preserving the distinctions between them. An illustration of this is found in Jean de Joinville's biography of the French king Louis IX. At Whitsuntide in 1260, Louis found himself in a gathering of nobles in Corbeil, where Robert de Sorbon, master theologian and chaplain to the king, told Joinville that he was not dressed correctly, since his clothes were more distinguished than the king's. (The monarch was simply dressed in black, whereas Joinville outclassed him in fur-trimmed clothes of gray and green.) Joinville replied that he had inherited these colors from his parents and was obliged by his standing to dress in this way. He then attacked de Sorbon, a peasant's son, for dressing far above his station by wearing expensive wool that was really only fit for a king. Joinville was a member of the old aristocracy: he came from Champagne, owned a good-sized castle and extensive lands, and bore the title of court-marshal.

All the provocative colors in public life created so much unrest that measures had to be taken. At the same time, a much broader cultural movement was under way, which called for distancing oneself from nature, controlling one's emotions, and creating a private domain. Silencing all those loud colors was perfectly in keeping with this movement, not only because color tended to advertise high birth but also because it was used increasingly to broadcast the strongest of emotions.

This was partly why both court and town switched to black and blue, a fashion that was ushered in by Louis IX. After his return from the Crusades, he tended to dress in simple fabrics dyed blue or black, doubtless in imitation of the clergy. The worldly elite, after all, followed eagerly in the footsteps of the great scholastics. Colorful clothing was denounced ever more frequently as an impotent display on the part of the nouveaux riches, who sought pleasure in an everyday life that they filled with gaudy colors. In 1494 the moralist Sebastian Brant complained in his book *Narrenschiff* (Ship of fools) that peasants were no longer content to wear gray smocks, preferring instead brightly colored worsted garments like those of the more worldly nobles and burghers. Moreover, young folk—according to Brant—were treating their hair with sulfur and resin and bleaching it in the sun to make it even more yellow.

Contemporaries considered the switch to dark colors in the higher circles to be connected with the great plague epidemics of the mid-fourteenth century. This unmistakable sign of God's wrath, which they felt could not go unheeded, gave rise to an atmosphere of penitence, resignation, reticence, and grief—and colors to match. This is testified to with a leaden heart in a late-fourteenth-century song from aristocratic circles in Bruges:

> A habit my heart now doth wear,
> It's black, the one it has put on.
> And underneath it, always there,
> A gray one it has chosen to don.
> How can my heart's cares e'er be gone?
> For black is mourning, gray is toil.
> From lust and mirth it doth recoil.

Explanations for this about-face must surely be sought in a broader context. Repentance, self-control, and the formation of an elite all played a role in this development. Black and blue became the colors associated with keeping a respectable silence, distancing oneself, and, in particular, retreating from public exposure. This is why the Holy Roman Emperor Charles V ordered black tapestries for his walls after his abdication in 1556. His royal household, however, soon put such melancholy contrition to good use by devising new ways to distinguish themselves. They had their black wall hangings and clothing made of the costliest silk—the perfect backdrop for precious stones of subtle colors. Just as long as there was no trace of color in the cloth itself!

Dark clothes lent dignity to the wearer, and black therefore became the uniform of the new cultured elite. Dark colors live on in modern-day tails and tuxedos and even in the blue of jeans, which have been adopted by the entire Western world as a kind of uniform, a way of advertising that the wearer enjoys an uncomplicated, informal lifestyle.

Well into the fifteenth century, however, a countermovement managed to create the bright color contrasts at which the Burgundian court excelled—except for the dukes themselves, of course, who remained faithful to the tendency of the *haute noblesse* to display a preference for black (indeed, Philip the Good wore no other color). Contemporaries sought an explanation for the colorfulness of society's lower echelons in the same plague epidemics that had supposedly sparked off the sudden predilection for black. In the wake of Boccaccio's *Decameron*, a penchant for frivolity had developed in the higher circles, a widespread feeling of "live and let live," of wanting to enjoy life despite hardship and setbacks. This movement also manifested itself in clothing, which not only glowed with bright colors but also exuded a rather aggressive and undeniably eroticizing joie de vivre. Sexual characteristics were provocatively displayed in revealingly low necklines and tight-fitting trousers and bodices.

By the end of the Middle Ages, however, decolorization had won. When color tried to seize power, it was thwarted by the much stronger movement toward personal aloofness, self-control, and concealment. Black and white, moreover, had been stripped of their powers of expression and dismissed from the color spectrum. Scientific evidence for this was later provided by Newton, who proved that black and white do not occur as colors in the spectrum but are instead states in which all colors are either absorbed or reflected. Nowadays many people do not think of black and white as colors, much like the fifteenth-century moralists and their predecessors.

The dominance of the black-white color scheme was furthered by the arts of bookmaking and engraving, which assumed a central place within the world of mass communication, reducing it to a display of light and dark. The colorful effects of stained glass, so essential to the medieval sense of beauty, were also toned down to earth colors, enlivened by some yellow. Sixteenth-century stained-glass windows—both sacred and profane—were dominated by shades of gray, brown, white, and yellow. The effect of the sun shining through them was to make the walls warmer and more earthly. Apparently, it was becoming less acceptable to see lightninglike flashes of contrasting color bursting through the church windows.

The atmosphere of decolorization, which was given a big boost by the Reformation and Calvinism and resisted in vain by romanticism, is the one we live in today. Only in the course of the twentieth century did color begin to make a cautious comeback, first in films, then in television and magazines. In daily life, we display a distinct preference for the softening effect of pastel colors. These toned-down hues show that we have no intention of returning to the colorful richness of the Middle Ages—except, of course, in occasional splurges that are obviously at odds with the colorless life of a routine day.

1. Sudden growth in popularity of the color blue: *Achilles Killing Hector*.
In *Roman de Troie,* by Benoît de Sainte-Maure, inv. no. 216, MS 66,
thirteenth century. 's-Heerenberg, Huis Bergh.

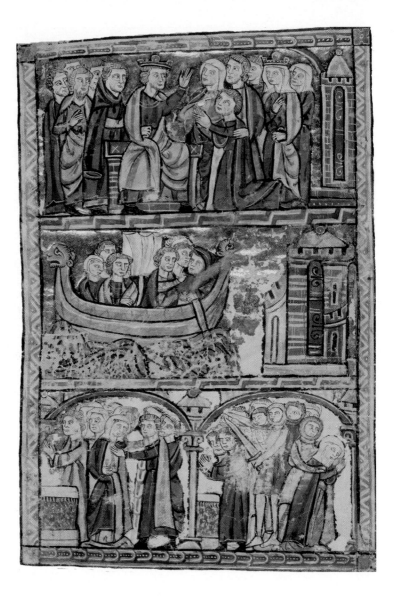

2. Dominance of the color blue: *Various Scenes from the Story of Troy*. In *Roman de Troie*, by Benoît de Sainte-Maure, inv. no. 216, MS 66, thirteenth century. 's Heerenberg, Huis Bergh.

3. Dominance of the color blue: *The Charity of Saint Nicholas*. MS *Images du Christ et des saints*, n.a.fr. 16251, fol. 90v, end thirteenth century. Paris, Bibliothèque Nationale.

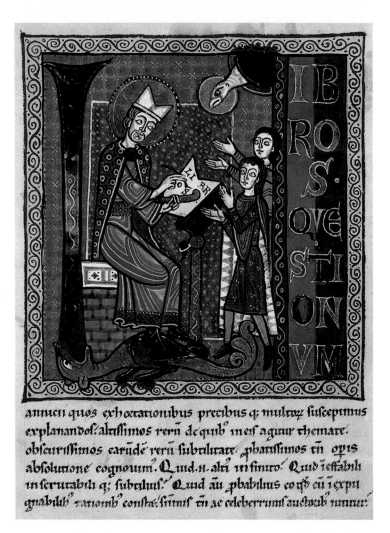

anmien quos exhoetationibus precibus q; multox suscepimus
explanandos. altissimos rerū dequib' in eis aguur rhemate.
obscurissimos earūdē rerū subtilitate. pbatissimos tn opis
absolutione cognouim. Quid.n. alti in sinuo? Quid ieffabili
in scrutabili q; subtilius. Quid au pbabilius eo qd cū i expu
gnabilib' rationib' constat. simul tn ae celeberrimis auctorib' niniti?

4. Structuralizing, contrasting colors without much specific meaning:
Bishop Gilbert de la Porrée (Poitiers) Writing a Commentary on Boethius.
MS O II 24, fol. 14r, ca. 1200, Basel, University Library.

5. Colors as contrast; the meaning is secondary: *Birth of Christ*. MS St.
Peter perg. 7, fol. 1v, 1230. Karlsruhe, Badische Landesbibliothek.

6. Colors as contrast, without any deeper meaning: *The Descent of the Holy Ghost.* Evangelistary, ca. 1150. Stuttgart, Württembergische Landesbibliothek.

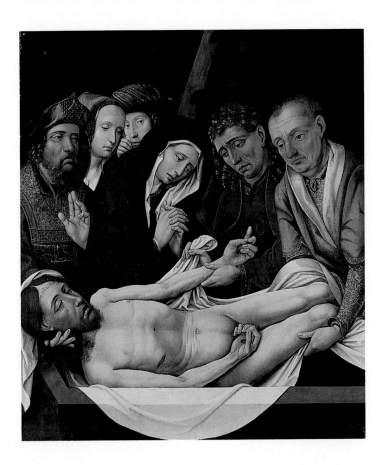

7. Discolored body (yellowish green) of the dead Christ: Colijn de Coter, *Entombment*. Inv. no. 4033, ca. 1500. Maastricht, Bonnefantenmuseum.

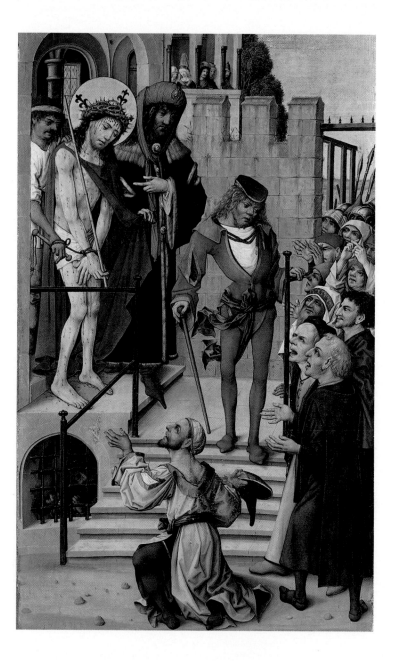

8. Jewish mocker of Christ in colorful clothing, predominantly yellow: *Ecce Homo*. Left wing (inside) of the Altarpiece of the Housebook Master, ca. 1470–1505. Freiburg im Breisgau, Augustinermuseum.

9. Flagellators of Christ in colorful clothing: Northern Netherlandish master, *The Flagellation of Christ*. Inv. no. 70.1, ca. 1460–70. Budapest, Szépmûvészeti Museum.

The left panel reads:

·PRÆMIA
SALTATRIX
POSCIT
·FVNEBRIA
VIRGO·
IOANNIS
CAPVT
ABSCSVM
QOD LANC
REPORTAT·

The right panel reads:

INCESTÆ
AD GRE·
MIVM MA·
TRIS FERT
REGA ÐNVM·
PSALTRIA
·RESPERSIS
MANIBVS
DE SANGV·
INE IVSTO·

10. Executioner portrayed in striped "half-breeches": circle of Lucas van Leyden, *Salome Receiving the Head of John the Baptist*, beginning of sixteenth century. Philadelphia Museum of Art, The John G. Johnson Collection, J-413.

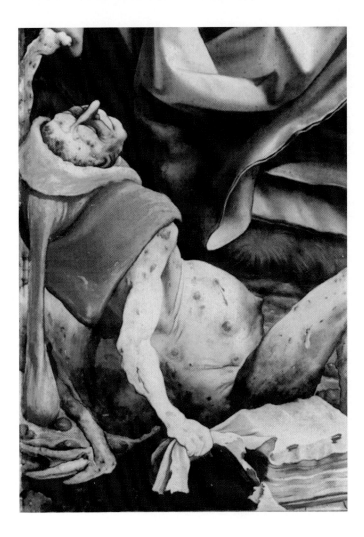

11. Warty devil-monster, exhibiting an extremely negative combination of colors—orange, red, yellow, green: Matthias Grünewald, *Isenheim Altar* (detail), ca. 1515. Colmar, Musée d'Unterlinden.

12. Greenish yellow Judas: fresco, end fifteenth century. La Brigue, Chapelle de Nôtre-Dame des Fontaines.

13. Green-and-yellow mocker of Christ: Johann Koerbecke, *Christ Before Pilate.* From Marienfelder Altar, inv. no. 382 1 m, 1457. Münster, Westfälisches Landesmuseum für Kunst und Kulturgeschichte.

14. Orange emphasizing Mary Magdalene's worldly past: Master of the Mansi Magdalene, *Saint Mary Magdalene*. Inv. no. 0076, ca. 1510–25. Maastricht, Bonnefantenmuseum.

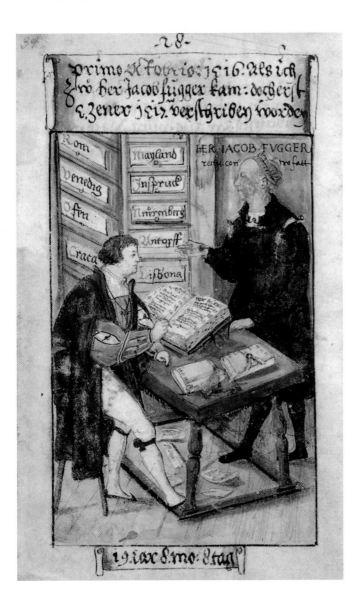

15. Green desktop and a merchant keeping his books, representing the vicissitudes of business: colored pen drawing, *Jacob Fugger in His Office*. In Matthias Schwarz, *Trachtenbuch*, ca. 1502–36. Braunschweig, Herzog Anton Ulrich-Museum.

16. Green-covered table and a game of cards, representing the fickleness of fortune: follower of Lucas van Leyden, *Card Players.* Inv. no. 923, first half sixteenth century. Budapest, Szépmûvészeti Museum.

17. Devils in various colors: *Le Livre de la Vigne Nostre Seigneur.* MS
Douce 134, fol. 99r, ca. 1450–70. Bodleian Library, University of Oxford.

18. Differently colored devils: fresco, 1365. Florence, Santa Maria Novella, Cappelone degli Spagnoli.

19. Black, the fashionable color for the upper nobility: Master of the Princely Portraits, *Lodewijk van Gruuthuse (Knight of the Order of the Golden Fleece)*, second half fifteenth century. Bruges, Groeningemuseum.

20. The wealth of color (partly owing to a nineteenth-century restoration of the original) in the twelfth-century abbey church of St. Austremoine in Issoire (Puy-de-Dôme).

CHAPTER THREE

Beautiful Colors for Mere Enjoyment?

In a way, the Middle Ages invented modern colors. This sounds strange, especially in light of the red in the wall paintings in Pompeii or the azure hippopotamuses of Egyptian antiquity. Generally speaking, though, before the late Middle Ages, colors were dull and drab: watery blue, for example, or such earthy hues as brown-red, pale yellow, and gray.

For the most part, this drabness was the work of time. We often find those faded earth and sea colors beautiful, because of the romanticism inherent in the old and weather-beaten. Bright colors did exist, of course, but they faded as soon as they were applied, which explains the paucity of such colors from that time. Furthermore, painters had long used tempera, which consists of pigments ground in water and then mixed—usually with egg yolk—just before use. It was difficult to render sharp contours and deep hues when working in tempera. The drying process was also a problem. Painted panels were set out in the sun to dry, but often the paint would crack where the wood had been joined. Experiments were therefore conducted to find other emulsion vehicles, at first with little success.

Then all at once—so sudden did it seem—in the fifteenth century, there appeared in the work of the Flemish painters the unctuous sheen and deep hues of oil paint. Jan van Eyck is credited with its invention, and to a certain extent this is true. Oil-based paints were already in existence, but Van Eyck was the first to develop a practical method of application, from grinding the pigments to drying the paint without the help of the sun. Oil paint proved to be more durable and to dry more quickly with less chance of cracking. It also produced warmer, more beautiful hues and greater color contrasts. It did not take long for others to fathom the secret of the Flemish Primitives, and in the course of the fifteenth century it was adopted by a host of painters, first in Italy and then in the rest of Europe.

But did the people of the Middle Ages find these colors as beautiful as we do? And did they voice any opinion on the subject? It has frequently been remarked that the spontaneous love of nature died out almost completely in this period. An affinity with nature and the desire to depict it had apparently become little more than a compulsory exercise, the products of which were based on conventional models and formulas. Not until the Renaissance was nature rediscovered and again brought to life, as the writers of antiquity had so ably done. To put it another way, the notion of a rebirth is strongly associated in our minds with the reemergence of an unbridled love of nature.

Indeed, much of the nature depicted in medieval miniatures and paintings seems stiff and schematic, relying heavily on the descriptions of the earthly paradise in Genesis and the enclosed garden in the Song of Songs. Medieval depictions of landscape were apparently either created in the image of these primal landscapes or intended as direct references to that higher, eternal reality. In literature, things were not much different. Knightly tales revolving around Charlemagne, King Arthur, and other heroes of classical and medieval lore hardly mention nature, let alone its colors. The few allusions we do find invariably refer to the same literary landscapes that crop up everywhere, all of which feature green grass, tall trees, sweet-smelling flowers, singing birds, gurgling brooks, the proverbial balmy breeze—and all of this preferably in a space no bigger than an orchard.

These parklike patches of natural beauty are also direct references to eternity, often providing the setting for courtly love scenes that take place against the timeless backdrop of the highest love of the Song of Songs: nature as a *locus amoenus*—a pleasance, or "lovely place"—the term used in poets' handbooks to denote the formula for such ideal landscapes. Again and again, the twelfth-century Dutch poet Hendrik van Veldeke presents this obligatory landscape when his poetry turns to love. Why did he not simply look out the window at the valley between Liège and Maastricht where he often stayed? Had he not wandered through that strange landscape of chalk cliffs, rushing water, and forests of bronze-green oaks?

These formulaic descriptions were naturally more exciting to van Veldeke's contemporaries than to us. However satisfying an immediately recognizable reference to eternity might have been, medieval painters and poets were particularly attracted to the variations they could bring to bear on such formulas when shaping their own art. This creative process, in which they revealed their mastery of the idiom, was of necessity dictated by the topicality of the subject and the wishes of their patrons. If a painter was severely restricted by the complicated meanings adhering to color, his particular skill would reveal itself in the way he artfully integrated the colors of his patron's coat of arms into a work of art without having to change its character.

There are so few firsthand accounts of people going into raptures at the sight of color or expressing admiration for a real-life landscape that can be located on a map that it is surprising to find a letter written by Petrarch in 1336 in which he gives a detailed description of a walk to the top of Mount Ventoux—an actual mountain in the Vaucluse. Petrarch is curious about this two-thousand-meter-high heap of bare stone. How does it affect the landscape, and what vistas can be seen from its peak? But on closer inspection it appears that Petrarch, too, seized on this experience of nature as an opportunity for spiritual contemplation. In retrospect, he felt that the whole enterprise smacked of vanity, and his struggle to get to the top despite losing his way so often was symbolic of humankind toiling to arrive without mishap in the next world.

❀

Why couldn't something simply be beautiful? There were many reasons for medieval man to keep a formal distance from nature on parchment and paper. The attitude was determined by two closely related notions about nature. The first consisted in the strong belief that God spoke to man through nature, thus revealing his intentions regarding Creation in general and humankind in particular. Nature was an open book, one that was easier and more straightforward to read than the Bible. The Bible also stated these intentions, but in a form reserved for the literate. Yet it was the task of every Christian to dedicate his fleeting earthly existence to the "reading" of both "books," with or without the help of priests and theologians—in other words, to undertake the quest for God.

The second notion was based on the belief that one must never forget nature's pitiful, polluted state since the Fall. Man had let himself be seduced into false beliefs, misled by the insolent assumption that God's power could be equaled. Should man, created in his likeness, not be privy to the same knowledge? This tempting idea was born of the vengefulness of the fallen angels. As devils doomed to eternal damnation, they had had every intention of dragging mankind down with them. And they would have succeeded, too, if Christ the Redeemer had not come to save the weak and the sinful, whose hopes of everlasting life depended on their continued belief and faith in God.

All the same, nature had been morally tainted since the Fall. It had truly become the devil's playground, a permanent threat and source of temptation, ever capable of bringing the world to rack and ruin. Life on earth, lasting only a fraction of a second in relation to all eternity, was portrayed as nothing more than a pilgrimage to the heavenly Jerusalem. To arrive there, man had to traverse an earthly path on which the devil had laid his snares in the most unexpected places. Man ran the gauntlet, stumbled, and fell; he was frail and sickly—this theme occurred over and over again in countless texts and images—and he was dependent both on his ability to reason and on the virtues, the gifts of the Holy Spirit. Personified as helpful figures, these virtues were willing to stand by him, provided he followed their advice to the letter.

Nature was not only a book from which to learn but also man's enemy. This coincided nicely with Germanic and Celtic beliefs, as well as with early medieval beliefs in demons. All that was inexplicable in nature—the devastation caused by hail, lightning, floods, failed harvests, and fires—was depicted in the guise of evil demons, dragons, and monsters. It was necessary to fight these destructive forces by invoking the name of demonized forefathers and kindly gods who might be able to help.

This explains the longstanding, deep-rooted tradition of man's struggle against nature and his tendency to turn away from it, as well as his corresponding need to describe and portray an idealized nature—nature as God had intended it, bursting with beauty and meaning. This true nature had revealed itself in the garden of Eden, which—even though its doors were closed to man—must have been situated somewhere on earth. This idealized nature, still so palpably present on earth, provided the basis for those stereotyped re-creations in art. That lost paradise figured prominently in the practices of various heretical movements. In particular, the Adamites (whose name is derived from the first man) sought nature in this ideal form: plenty of green, abundance, communal property, nudity, and carefree sex. In both literature and the visual arts, the ideal life was lived in a paradisiacal state of nature. Time and again, nature was admired and described in the state of perfection for which it was intended. And it was fervently believed that one day this perfection would again manifest itself on earth.

Did people in the Middle Ages really live in continual fear and awe of natural phenomena? Or was it also possible to enjoy and benefit from nature's bounty? After all, everything one saw, felt, or smelled could also be a reminder of that future paradise. And yet everything contained some moral significance. Even positive portrayals of the warmth of the sun in one's own garden and the beauty of the flowers in the nearby meadow were direct references to the cruel transience of such beauty. Like everything after the Fall, nature was transitory. Only in paradise was there no such thing as time or decay, and paradise was therefore the only place where beauty could exist. Nature was tainted, and its corrupting effect was responsible for encouraging the pilgrim in *Dat boeck van den pelgherym* (The book of the pilgrim)—a literary manual of virtues and vices—to stray from the straight and narrow by tempting him with colors, just as Dame Idleness, the daughter of Sloth, intended: "I guide the people who pass by here into the green meadows to pluck beautiful roses and other flowers, thus leading them to take great pleasure and delight in such splendid surroundings."

Nevertheless, we also find unmistakable evidence of emotional reactions to real-life experiences of nature in the Middle Ages, even though we are almost never told when and where they took place. Medieval notions of the corrupting influence of nature and references to the ideal doubtless still played a role, though they did not necessarily stand in the way of unmitigated pleasure. In his twelfth-century encyclopedia, the great Bartholomaeus Anglicus—with not a hint of didacticism or cautionary tale-telling—describes landscape as a source of human pleasure. And even though he refers continually to the recognized authorities of classical antiquity and the Middle Ages, there is the occasional outburst of pure pleasure, as when he writes about meadows: "Meadows give comfort to the eye through their verdure, to the nose through their smell, and they benefit man through their abundance."

Indeed, it is hard to deny that a contemporary of his, the abbot Hugo of St. Victor, was not also speaking from unmediated personal experience when he praised the glorious color green: "How it enraptures the minds of those who behold it, when new buds come forth in a new spring, and, rising like little darts, as if treading down death, burst into the light, an image of future resurrection." Yet this is not just an excited individual waxing jubilant. Hugo was trying to define a natural phenomenon from the perspective of eternity, which is why he did not refer to a concrete time or place but to a pattern in the divine order of things. The question of whether or not Hugo really found green "beautiful beyond any color" is unhistorical, because for him such a frame of reference did not exist. For Hugo, taking pleasure in an earthly phenomenon would have meant that the devil had him in his clutches. True beauty and the most profound pleasure consisted, after all, in being allowed to fathom God's order, with the help of the signs planted in nature for this very purpose.

Descriptions of distinct impressions of color are found once or twice in accounts of journeys to the Holy Land. Such guidebooks are actually much less original than one would think. Following the same pattern, they testify to having seen exactly the same things, both en route and at the destination itself. In this respect, they resemble modern travel guides, which also borrow freely from one another, even to the extent of appropriating other authors' personal impressions. Bertrandon de la Broquière, however, succeeded in his *Voyage d'Outremer* (Overseas voyage) in giving a candid account of the great pleasure afforded by the sight of cotton trees near Mount Tabor: "And it seemed—to those who did not realize that it was caused by the rising sun—as though snow had fallen on those cotton trees, for the leaves were as green as the leaves on grapevines, but with cotton on them." This comparison was not part of the standard repertoire of formulas used to describe natural phenomena. And even if he did borrow this impression of nature, the genuine excitement it conveys had at least been felt by the author of the source text.

It nonetheless remains difficult to find eyewitness accounts of the sensations produced by colors in specific locations. Apart from the fact that medieval man thought of color as an unavoidable blight on his perception of reality, he also believed that literature was not the appropriate place to recount idle impressions and emotions. Even if we assume that people in the Middle Ages could be just as moved by beautiful colors as we are, they would not have publicized this emotion in literature as we are used to doing. The same applies to visual art. Though its manifestations then and now are in many ways analogous, its underlying intentions, implications, and interpretations differ remarkably. In other words, our perception of the color of a strawberry differs from that of someone in the Middle Ages, no matter how lifelike the fruit embellishing the margins of medieval books of hours might seem.

Taking pleasure in nature in general and color in particular occurred in the Middle Ages in another sphere and was unfortunately almost never recorded on parchment or paper, so that direct knowledge of it remains elusive. And, as is often the case when hard evidence is lacking, this has led us to assume that in those days no one took a lively interest in nature. Nevertheless, the visual arts offer various clues in support of the theory that colors were used just as much or even exclusively because of their expressive value (see figs. 4, 5, and 6). Ottonian book illumination—referring to a period named after three German emperors called Otto in the tenth century—largely contradicts the notion that color was primarily intended to signify something. Although all the illustrations in question are religious in nature, the colors can scarcely be linked to any deeper meaning. There is a marked preference for cryptic colors such as violet, purple, lavender, and the more unusual shades of blue and green. Gold functions as a filler—as both stage and scenery. The background frequently consists of a field of gold—regardless of whether heaven, earth, or a wall is being depicted—making it seem as though the figures are being presented on a golden platter, in a heightened and accentuated form.

Colors used in this way have a strictly structural function within the depiction as a whole. They catch the viewer's eye and undoubtedly inspire and emphasize wonderment and awe, but they are devoid of meaning. In an evangelistary—a book containing a copy of the Four Gospels—made especially for him, Otto III (d. 1002) is portrayed with a blue robe, blue hair, blue shoes, vermilion hose, violet cloak, and a green sword with a golden hilt.

The colors have no symbolic meaning whatsoever, not on a deeper level and not as a reference to the natural colors of the objects and garments depicted.

There is an even more vivid example: an evangelistary produced around 1000 (now preserved in Brescia) at the most renowned book-illumination studio of this period, the scriptorium of the Abbey of Reichenau. The depiction of Christ's entry into Jerusalem is a wild fantasia of color apparently inspired by this holy event. Against a backdrop formed by a golden circle embedded in a field of purple, Jesus, wearing a purple cloak, comes riding up on a dark red donkey, with a lavender halo emitting orange-brown rays of light. His disciples and the young men in the crowd are dressed in red, lavender, purple, green, and pale yellow. The city of Jerusalem in the background is likewise a veritable symphony of color. The walls and towers are painted in all possible (and impossible) hues—dark green, light yellow, brick red, pink, lavender, and blue—and the roofs are covered with red tiles. This cacophony of color appears to be either a repeat performance of the scene in the foreground or an encore to the awe-inspiring motifs in the central representation.

In this case, the colors speak for themselves, lending the portrayal expression and making it more comprehensible, beautiful, and appealing. It is important to bear this in mind. Halfway through the Middle Ages, there emerged a solid tradition in the use of color that was diametrically opposed to the interpretations and uses of color in previous centuries. After this, the upstart tradition seems to have disappeared, as evidenced by the generous and ever-increasing use of color connotation from the twelfth century onward.

Nonetheless, the artistic production of the Ottonian era is as extensive as it is impressive. The pure color aesthetic it champions surely represents a school of thought that could neither have sprung up overnight nor disappeared without a trace. Perhaps this free use of color does not lend itself readily to theory and commentary. Nearly a thousand years later, we are forced to search for verbalized visions, extant sources—anything that people wrote down to ensure that it would not be lost. Or perhaps they were more interested in adding the weight of authority to certain viewpoints, or gathering contradictory arguments, or teaching things that were anything but obvious and commonplace?

On closer examination, it appears that Ottonian notions of color continued to exert an influence. In a miniature from a Cologne prayer book of around 1140, God sits in judgment on his throne. This rather simple theme prompted a loud splash of color in which the artist experimented with varying fields built up of ovals in combination with rectangles and leaf-shaped semicircles. Brightly contrasting colors, distributed rhythmically over the entire page, alternate within these lines. Here and there, a possible connection between the color and the figure or object suggests itself, but this is not essential to the color scheme. Other laws are at work here. Though God wears a basic white tunic, draped over it are garments in a wide variety of colors—blue, gold, and red—and he is crowned with a golden halo. The backdrop is a green oval, placed inside a blue oval, which is boldly outlined in red and white. Everywhere are golden stars, around which flutter green, red, blue, and pinkish brown leaves, interspersed with brown horses (displaying black spots), the whole edged in yellow and black, with another gold ground for the ovals. This is clearly an attempt to honor God with a magnificent profusion of color, and, according to twelfth-century notions, the best way to achieve this was to use bright hues and sharp contrasts. As a result, God practically leaps out of the deeply colored ovals and rectangles. This magnificence is amplified in medieval stained-glass windows. Here, resplendence reaches dazzling heights, continually revealing how colors are brought to life by light or how the divine breath infuses the earth with life every morning and withdraws again at night when its work is done.

This aestheticizing use of color as an end in itself can be found in late-medieval book illumination. Edges and frames are overgrown with intertwining leaves, plants, and animals. These illustrations display an odd mixture of almost oppressive verisimilitude and wild fantasies of nature that would be more at home in dream landscapes. Here, too, color strives primarily to produce an aesthetic effect and to provide structure, both of which are realized in complicated harmonies and striking discords. This also serves as a mnemonic device, since all that is memorable in a depiction can be associated with a specific color. Colors appear to imprint themselves on the brain more easily than the ideas associated with them. First and foremost, however, the true meaning of color is beauty, in which the divine also reveals itself.

❀

In the science and literature of the Middle Ages, colors are continually presented as variable expressions of meaning. In modern times, this has given rise to the idea that color must always be interpreted. In doing so, we still follow the rules laid down by all those medieval preachers and professors, perhaps even more diligently than their contemporaries did. But we run the risk of losing sight of other ways of looking at color, other attitudes that branch out in other directions and do not automatically interpret color as a reference to God's plan of salvation or, if they do, take the alternative route of harmony and beauty. Clearly, playing around with colors and their meanings was an exciting and entertaining pastime in the Middle Ages. Perhaps we should not take medieval attitudes so seriously. In any case, we should not view the results as a formalized expression of what all people saw, felt, and thought about color. Our overwhelming urge to interpret threatens to obscure our view of more expressive uses of color.

Everyone naturally takes pleasure in decorative colors, usually borrowed from nature and perhaps prompted by an object's natural appearance or by some symbolic meaning. But, first of all, there is the color itself, in all its ephemeral brightness, gradations, and brilliance. Background information and in-depth analyses properly belong on paper: *this* is what you should think about color, theologians and poets have always told us. Sometimes their writings are still aglow with the excitement they felt. It is easy to overlook this five or fifteen centuries later, but perhaps the embers of that fire will be enough to rekindle a feeling that was once a part of everyday life, an experience as intense as it was natural: an appreciation of the revelatory splendor of color.

CHAPTER FOUR

The Most Beautiful Colors Adorn the Woman

Even though the remarkable preference for blue and the equally striking aversion to yellow link us directly to the Middle Ages, there are curious differences between the medieval and the modern appreciation of color that are difficult to explain. Examples of this are to be found in the various ideals of feminine beauty.

The strong preference for blond hair belongs to every era. Golden hair was praised just as much in ancient times as it is nowadays. In the Middle Ages, too, women tried to live up to this ideal by dyeing their hair, or "yellowing" it, as a medieval poet described it. This blond ideal was just as prevalent in the north of Europe as it was in the south, regardless of the natural abundance or scarcity of blond hair. In areas boasting a plenteous supply of blondes, the degree of blondness determined the ideal.

An explanation of this really rather remarkable constant in the history of mores lies perhaps in the gold of the sun. This has been commented upon throughout the ages and forms the only counterbalance to the longstanding and widespread dislike of the color yellow. The gold of heavenly sunlight represents the only positive manifestation of yellow. Could it possibly be that those who have been touched to the very roots of their hair by these golden rays are privileged beings?

Apart from hair, however, there are no other constants determining the ideals of womanly beauty. Blue eyes were not part of the medieval ideal, whereas in our time they have an almost clichéd connection with blond hair. The medieval aversion to blue eyes probably harks back to classical antiquity, when blue eyes were reminders of the barbarians from the north. Women with blue eyes were thought to be wanton, while blue-eyed men were considered effeminate or even insane. Terence, a Roman writer of comedies, endowed his foolish characters with blue eyes and bright red faces. Green eyes were thought to be wicked, especially when combined with yellow hair, because this gave rise to the green-yellow color scheme indicative of folly or lunacy.

In the Middle Ages, blondes were supposed to have brown eyes and black—or at the very least dark brown—eyebrows. This combination, so strange to us nowadays, paved the way for hair-dyeing methods that enabled all those dark-eyed brunettes to achieve the ideal with relative ease. Why brown or black eyes, though? One can choose any reason one likes from the mind-boggling number of theories on offer. Medieval color symbolism practically works on demand, offering a limitless range of possible applications.

Brown is the color of the earth. This was immediately suspect, because the earth was also the devil's playground. Brown, moreover, stood for everything that was dark and sinister. On the other hand, the color brown could also express the utmost humility and a profound awareness of one's own mortality. In fact, it was usually taken to have the latter sense, viewed as a kind of noncolor that neutralized the habits of Franciscan monks and proclaimed penance, voluntary humiliation, and utter mortification.

The challenging combination of blond hair and brown eyes constituted an unusual contrast that was, for whatever reason, associated with the ultimate in beauty. Blond hair and brown eyes are, after all, a rarity among Western peoples. Except for this combination, though, brown and black were signs of extreme ugliness in women.

The Bruges poet Anthonis de Roovere (d. 1482) introduces in one of his "sottish refrains" a couple of elderly lovers, Pantken and Pampoeseken, who are planning to marry. De Roovere's verse mocks married love. The idea of romantic love between man and wife was a novel attitude that was rapidly gaining in popularity among the middle classes. In previous centuries, the bonds of matrimony had been more a matter of practical necessity. At any rate, the two lovers in de Roovere's refrain are as old as the hills and thoroughly disgusting, but their unattractive features are presented as attractions that fan the fires of love all the more. Pampoeseken wears a once-scarlet dress now blackened with soot. And the smoke from the cauldron has turned her hands "pepper-white."

Anna Bijns (d. 1575), the versifying schoolmistress from Antwerp, incorporates this subject matter in a couple of verses written for the benefit of her public, the local Franciscan monks, who were especially amused by her mockeries of marriage. In one of these refrains, a man complains of being tied down to an evil woman who is too ugly to look at: "Her loosely hanging hair was as black as coal." Similarly, another representative of the species not only has the same black hair but never even washes her hands: "She has two hard, black, coarsened hands. . . . This little goddess has black hair on a scabby head."

Black and brown were thought to be dirty in a woman, but in combination with blond hair—a blessing of the highest order—brown eyes expressed the utmost humility. Next, the model of feminine beauty demanded a red-and-white color scheme for the face. Or so we may conclude from the numerous descriptions of characters in chronicles, legends, and knightly tales that refer to a host of women—both worldly and religious—proudly led by the Virgin Mary.

In one of his poems, Jacob van Maerlant reflects in depth on the beauty of the Virgin Mother. Her hair is even more beautiful than golden thread, and her forehead surpasses the whiteness of a lily. Furthermore, she has dark eyebrows, eyes like carbuncles—precious stones of a fiery red or near-black color—cheeks that outshine red roses, white teeth, a neck whiter than a swan's, and white, delicately shaped hands.

This blond-dark, red-white ideal of feminine beauty occurs over and over again in medieval literature. Mary undoubtedly remains the most obvious point of reference, so much so that she even colors the image of her son. There is also a worldly model, however, which is presented in a Latin textbook on writing, *Ars Versificatoria (The Art of Versification)*, written around 1175 by Matthew of Vendôme. One section of this book offers descriptive models to be used in portraying people in print. Feminine beauty is personified by Helen of Troy, who has "golden hair." His praise unfolds thus:

> Her dark eyebrows, neatly lined twin arches,
> Set off skin that is like the Milky Way.
> With equal candor a blush that would make the captive
> Rose pay tribute suffuses her face. As it fades away,
> The blush proves no enemy to her face as rosy hue and
> Snow-white skin contend in most delightful combat.
>   . . .
> The glory of that countenance is her rosy lips . . .
> Those honied lips redden in laughter most delicate.
> Her teeth are straight and even, and their whiteness
> Like ivory. Her smooth neck and shoulders whiter than
> Snow give way to firm but dainty breasts.

Though these characteristics are constantly repeated and enlivened by new metaphors, the color scheme remains the same. A contemporary, Bartholomaeus Anglicus—writing in the field of science—decreed that the key to a woman's beauty is her complexion. He likewise maintained that facial beauty ought to consist in the harmonious alternation of white and red, indicative of a mixture of purity and warmth.

These ideals were by no means upheld exclusively by members of the artistic and scientific elite. Beautiful women in the oral tradition of popular culture also fit this description. A good example is the haughty princess in the age-old ballad of Master Halewijn. Before going to visit Halewijn, this princess puts on her best clothes: a gold-trimmed bodice and a gold skirt with gold buttons that set off to advantage her gorgeous blond hair, which is topped with a crown of gold. Naturally, she has clear brown eyes, as the rapist and murderer Halewijn just manages to observe before he is beheaded.

A daring variation on this theme is presented by the erotic ballad *Dmeisken metten sconen vlechtken* (The girl with the beautiful braids), a recitation jotted down for future performance around 1400. The writer longs for the girl who left him, whom he can conjure up for the listener only in the most seductive of terms. Her lips and face are redder than a rose could ever be, her teeth are like ivory, her body is as white as snow, her eyes burn like a lion's, her breasts are "rounder than a ball," and in her chin she has a comely dimple.

This last feature points the writer in the direction of his final destination, which he approaches—surprisingly enough—via her hair. En route, he leads the connoisseur on a delightful journey, starting with the desirable brown of her eyebrows and moving on to the hair under her arms and "down there," where she has "a little hole in her body" that he would prefer to call—if only he dared say it—her cunt: a subtle, poetic way of saying it without actually saying it. And now that the cat—or pussy—is out of the bag, he adds, "Brown-haired are the lovely loins of this girl." These virtuoso variations, which give the poet a chance to show off his technique, prove just how compelling these ideals of feminine beauty, immortalized in centuries of literature and visual art, actually were.

❁

In modern times, these points of reference no longer exist. Perhaps they continued to simmer below the surface in those powdered and rouged women of the eighteenth- and nineteenth-century aristocracy. For centuries, though, a white complexion was an important distinguishing feature—certainly for women—of the upper classes and later also of the well-to-do middle classes. Only an increasing appreciation of nature, coupled with a renewed interest in health, has caused this attitude to change in modern times. A suntan indicates physical well-being, and, even though this is suspect as a source of earthly pleasure, it is also desirable in the context of perfecting and completing the divine plan laid out for mankind. A sound mind lives in a sound body, and both feel most at home in their natural habitat: a suntanned face bears witness to this newfound bliss and the propitious influence of divine nature.

In the course of the twentieth century, healthy looks have also been exploited by members of the new elite as a means of rising above the rabble. Skiing in the Alps or sunbathing on the shores of the Mediterranean were, until recently, pleasures reserved for the upper classes and the more prosperous members of society, and the suntans they brought home with them bore witness to their privileged position. In recent decades, however, a suntan has begun to lose its positive connotations, primarily because it has been democratized and is now within everyone's reach. The tanning bed quickly met a similar fate, and a suntan thus obtained has also lost its glamour. Those sunburned faces and bleached heads of hair, acquired by overdosing on Alpine sun, are inevitably making suntans less exclusive and therefore less desirable.

Moreover, while a suntan used to be sought for reasons of health, this motive has been swept away in recent years by doctors' warnings against prolonged exposure to ultraviolet rays. Tan, therefore, is going out of fashion as a bodily color. Even so, white has not yet made a comeback. A lusterless light brown, easily achieved by applying make-up, now seems to be the best bet.

A sunburned face was considered ugly in the Middle Ages. Everything dark—except for the eyes—was a direct reference to the beastly state of man, his earthbound nature, and his apparent inability to free himself from it. A suntanned face was an instant advertisement of these undesirable ties to nature, the outdoor life, and the necessity of working the land. In a list of everything that was bad, the Antwerp poetess Anna Bijns names a "brown face with freckles." There's practically nothing worse, for a spotted or mottled complexion was considered even more objectionable than a uniform tan—an aggravated form, as it were, of an already repulsive condition. Freckles, moreover, were thought to be a sign of having been sinfully conceived during menstruation.

Only one type of person was exempt from the aversion to a sun-tanned face and that was the war hero. His face was supposed to be brown, otherwise he might be suspected of hiding at home to avoid the dangers of battle. Jacob van Maerlant therefore endowed the nearly perfect Hector of Troy—he lisps a bit and is slightly cross-eyed, but these trifling imperfections are hardly notice-able—with brown skin that can compete with the obligatory brown eyes of beautiful people.

It was even thought that brown-skinned warriors—not innately brown, of course, but tanned on the field of battle—were the most valiant. The countless stories, adapted for high-born and low-born alike, of the sack of Jerusalem in 70 A.D.—God's ultimate vengeance for the murder of his son—feature a man of exemplary coloring in the Roman army who was chosen to be the instrument of God's retribution. The Jews' resistance continued unabated, despite a protracted siege that made them wild with hunger. According to one text, printed in Gouda in 1482, the army searched hard to find a man to be the first to scale the walls. He was to be rewarded so generously that every soldier would envy him. No one volunteered, however, "except one knight among those present, by the name of Silvius and born in Syria, a brave, brown, and muscu-lar man." That "brown" actually says it all: this is a man to be reck-oned with, not one to be chased off the battlefield.

Very subtle indeed is the tension created between the acceptable brown of the brave warrior and the objectionable coloring of the peasant as reported—or rather called into question—in the description of Mordred, a knight of the Round Table. It is precisely such elitist literature that shows off the author's ingenuity by dis-paraging the brown complexion of the ruffian among the princi-pal players. According to the Middle Dutch version of the legend of King Arthur, Mordred figures as an outstanding liegeman, at least as far as his physique is concerned. He is in fact considered the world's handsomest knight, not least because he is "a bit brown."

That "bit" is especially intriguing: too much would make him a country bumpkin, too little the butt of courtly jibes. But there is more to it than meets the eye, for Mordred proves—despite his seemingly perfect looks—to be a villain, an archimpostor. A bit too brown after all?

In a great many instances, having a tan face or brown skin was wholly unacceptable. It is therefore inconceivable that people living in the Middle Ages would ever have sunbathed or in any way deliberately exposed their skin to the sun. Indeed, civilization was leading away from nature and calling increasingly for the suppression of earthly desires and bonds. This tendency found expression not only in clerical vows of chastity but also in the ideals promulgated by the new elites forming among the aristocracy and bourgeoisie.

That, at least, was the norm, as witnessed by sources many and various. Once in a great while, however, we run into a text that doesn't care a whit about Church doctrine or scholarly precepts. Then, quite simply, people showed their emotions and submitted to the reality of experience, which in earlier times had proclaimed that being at one with nature was in some respects a legitimate condition. At such moments, sunbathing becomes perfectly acceptable, and consequently "a brown color in the face indicates good health." This is how it is put in a popular didactic manual treating the female body, printed around 1538 in Utrecht, titled *Der Vrouwen Natuere ende Complexie* (Of women's nature and complexion). Sometimes, simple well-being takes precedence over erudition.

Otherwise, though, it's white and red all the way. This color scheme, so compellingly cataloged in writings on the Virgin Mary and Helen of Troy, occurs repeatedly in portrayals of beautiful women. Popular culture has its Snow White and Little Red Riding Hood, who embody feminine beauty and chastity. Galiene, the beloved of Ferguut of the Round Table, fits this description perfectly. Moreover, in the Middle Dutch version of the *Roman de la Rose* (*The Romance of the Rose*)—the long-drawn-out allegory of love that took Europe by storm from the fourteenth century onward—the personification of Joy is a beautiful woman with a white forehead, brown eyebrows, dark eyes, lips red as roses, and long blond hair.

Women who boast such magnificent coloring are lethal. Thus equipped, they arouse all sorts of desires, as Karel van Mander says in *Den grondt der edel vry schilder-const* (Foundation of the noble, liberal art of painting) of 1604, and these desires have driven men to wage full-scale war; Helen of Troy (whom he undoubtedly has in mind) is reduced to the ideal color scheme. The heroes who deserve to be admired, he continues, are those who have managed to suppress their desire for beautiful female bodies: "And in order to avoid looking at women with beautiful coloring, some have chosen blindness, because they feared losing control of their passions." Medieval *exempla*—a treasure trove for the writers of lay sermons—provide us with a wholesale supply of self-mutilation anecdotes, in which monks and nuns take drastic measures to rid their weak bodies of vulnerable ports of entry and erratically functioning organs.

It is not difficult to recognize in these timeworn descriptions the recurrence of conventions that were of decisive importance in shaping the older literature, even though the variants can be just as revealing. It was precisely this ingenious ability of the medieval poet to take stock ingredients and concoct a new flavor within the context of the story he was cooking up that offered possibilities for the best in pleasurable stimulation that literature was capable of providing.

In his *Historie van Trojen* (History of Troy), Jacob van Maerlant gives detailed descriptions of the outward appearance and the personality traits—which, according to medieval doctrine, are closely related—of the most important characters. Maerlant considers Polyxena, the daughter of King Priam, the most beautiful among women, which is why he takes great pains to apply the formula in such a way that she rises head and shoulders above the others. He announces his intention by opening with the statement that even if he were to write for a whole year he would not be able to do justice to Polyxena's beauty.

The example he follows in this endeavor is the French novel on Troy by Benoît de Sainte-Maure. At first, Maerlant stays within the confines of Sainte-Maure's scheme: Polyxena is white and has long blond hair, a white face, and blushing cheeks. Everything is compared to lilacs and roses. Then he begins to stray slightly from the model by attributing to her neck and bosom a whiteness that is even more blinding than the white of freshly fallen snow. The connoisseurs among his readership will recognize the variation here as being the freshness and unspoiled nature of that snow, which has just whirled down from the sky; snow as such is a familiar criterion. This is followed by an elaboration. He applies the tried and tested red-white color scheme even to her fingernails, describing her as having "long arms, hands, and fingers, and fingernails of white suffused with red."

In yet other texts, true literary ingenuity hits on the brilliant idea of applying the red-white color scheme to a female throat of such transparent whiteness that one could see red wine passing through it. And this image took root so firmly that it became part of the standard repertoire of literary models of beautiful women.

Nonetheless, there were times when a poet shunned convention and was moved by personal inspiration and excitement to recount what he himself found beautiful in a woman. Such spontaneous testimonials were rare in the Middle Ages, however, for literature was not considered the appropriate channel for outpourings of this kind. Moreover, developing emotional attachments to nature was merely asking for trouble, as this playground of the devil was a minefield, ever ready to bombard the senses with womanly beauty. A writer who displayed any sign of palpable excitement induced by real-life feminine beauty was automatically suspected of being possessed by the devil.

Furthermore, all things new or original—any obvious deviations from the accepted rules and established order—were equally suspect. Everything in the world was God-given and laid down for all eternity in Creation and the Bible. It was the poet's task merely to expound and explain what was already familiar and understood. The Fall of Man had made this necessary, for since then man had lost sight of the divine order of things, just as he had lost control of his emotions and senses. This had left the door wide open for the devil, who could permanently confound—from the inside out—any attempt to arrive at true understanding. New ideas were not considered a possibility, only new explanations of things forgotten, obscured, or corrupted.

It is difficult to imagine a time when originality as such was not acknowledged but sought instead in the creative treatment of existing formulas and material. It is only in the light of these theological conditions that one can understand why a poet would compose his descriptions of nature by recasting conventional themes. It was all the more remarkable, therefore, when a writer forcibly broke the mold. This occurs in a few Celtic texts dating from the early Middle Ages. Any suspicion that the isolation of that Irish backwater was to blame for such rebelliousness can instantly be allayed by taking note of the knowledge of literary tradition these writers so obviously possessed.

In the ninth century, the age-old story was recorded of the illustrious Irish king Eochaid, who went out riding and, chancing upon Etain—who was about to wash her hair beside a spring—was instantly captivated by her beauty. The text then launches into a very detailed description of Etain's breathtaking beauty as seen through the eyes of Eochaid. The leitmotiv of this long passage consists of colors, which figure in a number of bizarre comparisons and impressions. Etain uses a silver comb inlaid with gold. Her washbasin, also of silver and decorated with four golden birds, has gleaming, dark-red carbuncles set into its rim. Pinned to her cloak are silver brooches with ornaments of gold. Her tunic is made of green silk with red-gold embroidery. She wears her golden hair in braids, in four tresses, each adorned with a bead: "The color of her hair seemed to men like the flower of the wild iris in summer or like burnished red gold. There she was, loosening her hair to wash it, her arms out through the opening at the neck of her dress. White as the snow of a single night were her upper arms, tender and even, and her clear, lovely cheeks as red as the foxglove on the moor. Dark as the back of a stag beetle her two eyebrows; her teeth were like a shower of pearls in her head. Blue as the hyacinth were her eyes; her lips, red as Parthian scarlet." The list goes on to include straight, smooth, soft white shoulders; long hands; flanks as white as the crest of a wave, not to mention slender, long, smooth, and soft as wool; warm, smooth thighs, sleek and white; small, round, firm white knees; short, white, straight shins; and so on and so forth, complete with "a dimple of sport in both her cheeks, now flushed with purple red as a calf's blood, now bright with the luster of snow." Etain is known far and wide as a paragon of feminine beauty, and everything that can possibly be beautiful in a woman is measured against the standard set by her. The top-to-toe description is recognizable rhetorically as the nearly compulsory convention used in describing people. Hair the color of burnished red gold is a literary convention dating from antiquity, while the red-white color scheme of the Middle Ages is already looming in the background, emerging this time in the white of one-day-old snow.

The desire Etain arouses in King Eochaid is instant. He immediately gives himself away by telling her his name and inviting her to share his bed. Clearly, the writer has done his utmost to lend substance to Etain's indescribable beauty, which is why he deviates from the conventional imagery, with which he is obviously familiar. This is indeed daring, for he runs the risk of alienating his public. He is prepared to pay the price, however, because this is his way of making Etain very special indeed. And despite his eccentricity, everything seems to indicate that his enraptured description was well received. This text must have been transmitted for centuries in both oral and written traditions before it was finally given literary shape by a monk. At many points along the way, undesirable or unimaginable particulars could have been erased or replaced by the usual formulas. Perhaps this did occur to some extent, for by no means do all the details describing Etain deviate from the standard literary traditions adhered to since classical antiquity.

Perhaps the cross-fertilization of the great European literary traditions resulted in the hybrid implants of Christianity in these old Irish texts. Though Celtic in origin, they were not written down until centuries later, and then by tradition-conscious monks, who soon found it necessary to make a number of changes in both moral content and narrative form. Elsewhere, too, it is evident to what extent influences from antique and Christian written traditions have made inroads in these originally Celtic texts. Deirdre—the most beautiful girl in Ireland, who was to wreak havoc among the sons of Usnach—has blond curly hair, rosy cheeks, snow-white teeth, and fiery red lips: virtually a twofold version of the red-white color scheme for the ultimate in feminine beauty. Her eyes are gray-blue, however, a rather unusual variant on the customary brown of beauties. Still a young girl, she describes the ideal man she pictures as her future love: "Hair like a raven and cheeks like blood and a body like snow." This unintentional enumeration of the three dominant colors in the medieval scheme of things—red-white-black—also reveals that black hair in men was not necessarily unbecoming, as it was in women.

Such conventions cropping up even in these Christianized old Irish texts make the sudden variations in the description of Etain all the more striking. Between the approved models of beauty and their subtle variants there peers out from time to time a spontaneous expression of personal excitement, which not infrequently manifests itself in terms of color, pure and simple. At such times meaning coincides with beauty. There is nothing more medieval than that.

CHAPTER FIVE

The Devil's Pernicious Palette

Bernard of Clairvaux was not the only one who railed against the penchant for color, a tendency as exaggerated as it was dangerous. The notion that colors in all their earthliness were tools of the devil is actually as old as Christianity itself. Much depends on whether color is thought to be the refraction of light or a substance in its own right. Seen as the latter, it can indeed be considered a devious addition to Creation, one that obfuscates the true nature of things. If this is the case, then color is no more than an earthly ornament and, as such, can only be the work of the devil.

At the beginning of the sixth century, Pope Gregory the Great formally recognized the deceptive quality of color: "Foolish are those who let themselves be taken in by the colors of a depiction, thereby losing sight of the subject portrayed." This gave rise to the idea that the true nature of color is expressed by the word itself, "*color*" supposedly being a derivation of "*celare*," to hide.

Nearly ten centuries later, this problem was still far from being solved. The popular *Blason des couleurs* (Blazon of colors) attempted to arrive at a compromise by defining color as a "substance of light," inherently beautiful in itself but also representing a tangible addition to an object. This definition shows that the writer was out of his depth, which is why he so doggedly persisted in trying to demonstrate the usefulness and beauty of such enrichment. For one thing, color enables us to distinguish one object from another more easily.

Color also gives pleasure to those who perceive it, as well as bestowing power, beauty, and value on what it colors. And, last but not least, color lends people identity, security, and strength.

This plea, however, voiced at the very end of the Middle Ages, was an indication of the tenaciousness of the negative attitudes to color, rooted as they were in a tradition as old as the Church itself. As early as the second century, the Christian writer Hermas, author of *The Pastor of Hermas*, described how the celestial church gradually evolved from the earthly church. Using the parable of building a tower, he told how maidens—the helpers of God's only Son and the embodiment of his powers—carried building blocks of various colors, hewn by men from the surrounding mountains, to a tower under construction. As the stones were set in the tower, they turned shining white. Yet some of them kept their original color and could not be used, because they had not passed through the hands of the maidens.

The meaning of this parable is clear: radiant white was the color of divine light, while the other colors represented earthly existence and therefore had to be purified before passing over into the eternal life of heaven. Colors were eminently suited to represent the earth, whereas white light was ungraspable and otherworldly. In a scientific sense, too, most theologians and scholars came to believe, as the Middle Ages progressed, that as soon as pure light was refracted by an earthly substance, a spectrum of color was created. This belief was just one step away from interpreting color in a negative sense as yet another plaything of the devil.

To decolor, therefore, was to make immortal. This could even take place in stages. The same Hermas described the biblical monster Leviathan as having a head of four colors: black, blood-red, gold, and white. Ecclesia—the embodiment of the Church, presented in the guise of an ageless woman robed in white—explained that black represented the physical world, blood-red the future destruction of this world, gold the flight from earthly existence, and white the eternity in which God's chosen will dwell, immaculate and pure.

This is the sense in which white—black's constant companion

(and, since the seventeenth century, not considered a color, either)—has continued to be thought of to the present day. The white of distinction fits in nicely with the color's predominantly divine associations, while the negative term "colorless" refers more to gray and ashen than to pure white. The white flag of surrender expresses a state of purity, of sinlessness. In the past, hospitals hung out a white flag to report that no one had died that day, and a white flag flying from a prison was a sign that the cells were empty. Heavenly paradise, celestial robes, and the angels themselves all appear in white, which continues to set the tone for distinguished, candle-lit table settings. White signifies ultimate purity in every respect. This explains how even Christ could act as the great decolorer, who freed Creation from troublesome accretions of color. Thus the apocryphal Gospel of Philip says: "The Lord went into the dye works of Levi. He took seventy-two cloths of different colors and threw them into the vat. He took them out all white. Thus saith the Lord, 'Even so is the Son of Man come as a dyer'"—or, in this case, a bleacher.

Is this why underwear continued to be white for so long during the Christian era? Desire defiles, while immaculate white expresses cleansing and deliverance. It is more difficult to explain why campers and trailers are almost invariably white, or at least a pale beige reminiscent of white. Their very association with vacation should be enough to prompt a host of cheerful hues, completely in keeping with the vivid colors typically encountered on the road.

Perhaps the explanation is prosaic. Trailers began as vehicles used for traveling to the sun, and many sun seekers prefer white, for the simple reason that it offers more protection against the heat than black. Meanwhile, however, people have started taking to their trailers in all sorts of wind and weather, and present-day models offer much better protection against extremes of heat and cold. Yet white persists, as conventions so often do, long after their original purpose has faded into oblivion.

What usually happens is that the object takes on a new meaning, which continues to be largely implicit and can even assume mythical or symbolic forms. The white recreational vehicle has become the emblem of the inviolability of the ever-expanding private domain in the Western world. In this sense, the vacation house on wheels is an extension of the private home, a statement of its basic function, which is by definition limited in space. Entering that realm presupposes the greatest intimacy, which is why such vehicles are equipped with protective armor in the chaste color of maidens.

To the medieval mind, colors were earthly and therefore wrong. This was why even white, provided it was considered a true color, could also have a negative side: after all, colors—by virtue of their earthly, post-Fall taint—belonged to the demonic domain of vices and sin. This usage also recalls the "pale" horse in the Book of Revelation—"and his name that sat on him was Death, and Hell followed with him"—who comes to announce the final battle with the Antichrist. Finally, in late-medieval literature, white headscarves denoted whores, or at the very least wanton women, who can be recognized as such in various paintings by Hieronymus Bosch.

The anticolor campaign continued to be the focus of theological debate. The great Bernard of Clairvaux fought a lifelong battle against the deceptive provocation of color, whose allurements were apparently too great a temptation to what he thought of as morally handicapped humanity. Worst of all, of course, was that the devil had even found his way into the Church: "One puts on display a beautiful picture of a male or female saint, and the more powerful the colors of the portrayal, the more saintly one finds the portrayed." Bernard therefore provided his Cistercian order with a strong spiritual foundation that was proof against every form of color or adornment, which is why, to this day, their monasteries are white, bare, and immaculate. A church was supposed to be dark and dusky, without the distractions of light and color. Even the churches in Thomas More's *Utopia* of 1516 were "all somewhat dark." They were deliberately built this way on the advice of the priests, who found "overmuch light" a distraction to thought and considered "dim and doubtful light" an aid to focusing attention on divine service and prayer.

Hugo of Folieto was incensed at the rich decorations in buildings dedicated to God, the adornment of which was considered a necessary part of devotion. This twelfth-century prior of the Abbey of St. Laurent at Amiens was especially enraged by the painted rooms in episcopal palaces: "There, the statues are hung with colorful garments of great value, while, at the same time, a naked pauper with an empty stomach begs at the door. Depicted on the walls are Trojans dressed in purple and gold, but a poor Christian has no right even to rags. The Greek army is equipped with weapons, and Hector carries a shield of gleaming gold, but the poor beggar at the door is not even given bread, and, worse still, the poor are often exploited in order to clothe images of wood and stone!" Nor should a convent or monastery be painted: "Genesis should be read in the Bible, not on the wall." Saint Bernard parrots Hugo's very words when he links richly painted churches to the destitute who knock at the door in vain: "The church has magnificent walls but nothing for its poor; it wraps its stones in gold but lets its children run naked; the needy are forced to relinquish that which serves to delight the eyes of the rich."

In general, though, the discussion of the wickedness of colors focused more on clothing than on buildings or sculpture. As early as the mid-eleventh century, some prelates began to preach against the opulent clothing of clerics, later finding support in ecclesiastical edicts and episcopal decrees. Twelfth-century sources show that the dispute centered on costly materials with flaming colors, especially red. Green was also targeted as an undesirable color for clothing; later on, yellow was added to the list. The Fourth Lateran Council explicitly forbade the clergy to use "red and green textiles for any article of clothing whatsoever." Beginning in the thirteenth century, similar restrictions began to emerge in the secular sphere as well, especially in the cities, where some of these laws remained in force until well into the eighteenth century. The resolution of the Lateran Council even had an immediate effect on the statutes enacted in 1323 that forbade residents of the Antwerp *beguinages*—establishments housing Beguines, or lay sisters—to wear cloaks or jackets dyed red or green.

Outbursts such as those of Bernard of Clairvaux, who let fly at feminine beauty that depended on the deceitful donning of finery and colors, formed an important breeding ground for anticolor legislation. Such reproaches acquired a permanent place in the confession manuals and catalogs of virtues and vices, usually under the heading of vanity but also whenever pride or lust were the subject of discussion. One such didactic manual for the laity was the *Spiegel der sonden* (Mirror of sins), whose discussion of pride left no room for doubt that extravagant colors in clothing were very wicked indeed.

In clothing mankind, the author explained, God had had only two colors in mind, black and white, just as there were only two possible paths to be taken in earthly life, one sinful and the other virtuous. This was followed by a strong argument, which cropped up elsewhere as well, against dyed clothing: if colorfulness had been God's intention, he would have created sheep in a range of fashionable hues. After all, God had proved himself capable of producing great colorfulness, as evidenced by the riotous profusion of flowers on earth.

The author then focused his attention on women, creatures as wanton as they were sophisticated, who managed quite simply to make a virtue of necessity and turn the restrictions on colorful clothing to their advantage. According to the Bible, a woman's sense of modesty should require her to keep her head covered. There were, however, women who transformed their headscarves into attractive and seductive articles of clothing and even paraded them around provocatively in public. Yellow headscarves, in particular, came in for the severest censure. If these women thought that yellow suited them so well, why didn't they paint their faces a saffron color? White was the most suitable color for women, reflecting the color of God and the angels. Just imagine the heavenly hosts appearing in yellow!

Similar complaints about the excessive colorfulness of clothing and the use of makeup occur time and again in other texts as well. Cosmetic improvements were seen as tampering with Creation, as acts born of vanity, one of the devil's favorite instruments and bound to lead to ruin. In this context, once again, a ubiquitous image was that of the poor beggar who could live off what others daubed on their faces or decked themselves out in.

Changing color was thought to be the work of the devil and a direct assault on God's Creation, which was not intended to be other than it was. In the thirteenth century, in the *Rinclus*, a moralizing work that addressed the laity in the vernacular, Gielhijs van Molhem vehemently condemned the irreverence committed by women who painted themselves:

> There's no doubt about it: women who cover their faces with makeup, thereby besmirching the appearance God gave them, are only trying to wheedle Creation out of God's hands. . . . Like a potter, God created every human form individually according to his lights. Woe betide the woman who deliberately disregards that and tries to redo and recolor his work. That is like trying to sit on God's throne in order to make one thing better and destroy another. This is precisely what God looks upon with sorrow. A fully painted face is abhorred by God, for he wants his works—whether white or saturated with color—to remain as he made them.

These convictions add another dimension to the fourteenth-century farce *Die buskenblaser* (The box blower). An old peasant, ugly as sin, who cannot satisfy the needs of his young wife, goes to a quack to ask for a remedy. By applying a bit of color, he hopes to pass for a much younger man. He has come to the right person, the quack says, for he is an expert in rejuvenation cures. If desired, he will magically transform the elderly peasant into a real stud, "with black hair, and hot-blooded to boot." This was exactly what the peasant was hoping for: to rid himself of his gray hair as soon as possible.

At the next treatment, for which the peasant pays a princely sum, the quack repeatedly affirms the great transformation in color that can be expected: "If you blow into this box, you will turn an entirely different color." A perfect example of truth in advertising, since the box is filled with soot. "It will change your color," the quack promises, "and you will once again have a clear voice." No sooner said than done, and later on, at home, the peasant's young wife can indeed confirm that his face is no longer shining white but dirty black.

Such colorful facial transformations—including those produced by makeup—occur repeatedly in medieval literature, symbolizing the kind of diabolical behavior that undermines Creation. In the *Historie van Jason* (Story of Jason) of around 1360, it is the wicked king of Slovenia who sets to work in this way. He is in love with the beautiful Mirro, but she rejects him. He then requests an audience, which is granted. He cunningly decides to pose as someone else and consequently gathers some herbs "with which he covers his face so that he changes color." He is unmasked, however, and subsequently pursued with hue and cry. This king plays the part of a villain, completely in keeping with his dastardly metamorphosis.

The great mystic Jan van Ruusbroec gives a detailed account of how the devil uses his paint brush to seduce even nuns: "It is true that the devil has set new snares for the proud and haughty. That which should be black appears to be painted brownish red. The gray, undyed habit has taken on a blend of blue, green, and red. No tricks can be played with white; it has to stay as it is. Regardless of the color, however, one chooses the best wool to be had in the marketplace, despite one's social standing."

His worldly contemporary Jan van Boendale puts the clerical dispute in perspective, however, by remarking that the color of clothing has nothing to do with true devotion. He emphasizes this in *Jans teestye* (John's testimony), a long rhyming text in the form of a debate on the vicissitudes of life. Each monastic order seeks salvation in its own way. In doing so, one order wears gray, another black, and yet another white. But what difference does it make in the end? "One can lead a virtuous life in all kinds of clothes, whether variegated, green, red, blue, white, or gray; the hood does not make the monk any more than the hat makes the canon."

Jacob van Maerlant, an important source of inspiration for Jan van Boendale, stressed that it was wrong to attach too much importance to color, because the true nature of an object lay elsewhere. In doing so, he was engaging in a polemic with all those exacting Church scholars who were always at pains to point out that it was precisely those diabolical colors that obscured the true nature of things. But what does it matter, says Van Maerlant in a violent outburst aimed at the monastic orders: "Ultimately everyone ends up in the hellhole, whether dressed in blue, gray, black, or white."

Enlightened remarks such as these were completely in keeping with the spirit of the *Roman de la Rose* (*The Romance of the Rose*), in which a man wearing the habit of a Franciscan friar is presented as the personification of False Seeming. Claiming to live "in the world or in the cloister . . . but more in one and less in the other," he disparages "those false religious, wicked scoundrels who wish to don the habit of religion but will not subdue their hearts. . . . They call themselves poor but they are fed with fine, delicious morsels and drink precious wines; they preach poverty to you while fishing for great wealth. . . . You must look at my actions, if your eyes have not been put out, for if people do not act as they speak, they are certainly deluding you, whatever clothes they are wearing."

He is interrupted at this point by Love, who suspects impertinence. Does this mean that religion can be found outside the monastery? Of course, says the mendicant friar, who is living proof that the opposite is also true. "It does not follow that people lead a wicked life and therefore lose their souls because they are attached to worldly clothes; that would be a great sorrow. Holy religion can indeed thrive in colored clothes." False Seeming goes on to say that just as a wolf in sheep's clothing is no less likely to devour the ewes, so are saints in worldly clothing no less saintly in their behavior. These words, however, were put into the mouth of a suspect friar, so were they intended, after all, to be doubly ironic?

The German mystic Heinrich Seuse (Suso) highlights the wicked earthliness of color by portraying Jesus on the cross in all the colors of the rainbow: "Look, how Love has reddened, greened, and yellowed him!" These words refer at the same time to the negative connotations usually associated with multiple colors in appearance or clothing.

Seuse may have made Jesus' corpse very vivid indeed, but earthly encroachment through discoloration did in fact belong to the standard repertoire of poignant descriptions of his death (see fig. 7). In a Middle Dutch text on the life of Jesus, Mary stands at the foot of the cross, weeping for her dead son. His white body has turned completely black, his white teeth yellow. Mary was so accustomed to the once-white body that she cannot get used to the awful discoloration: "How steadily the blood flows from your wounds, from your white body; but dear son, why did I say that? I said that your skin was white. It used to be, but now it is all black." His earthly death has caused Jesus' body to take on the colors of putrefaction, and, in their very variety, these colors are indicative of temporality and transience. In the twelfth century, the learned encyclopedist Bartholomaeus Anglicus defined colors in terms of their mutability: they change in accordance with the heat of the sun and thus with the passing of time. To illustrate this, he pointed to the color of fruit: "First fruits turn green, as seen in grapes and mulberries, then they change into red, and finally they become whitish or black."

Fading and multicoloredness are symbolic of earthly things from which all traces of the divine have disappeared. Near the village of La Brigue in the southern French Alps lies the chapel of Nôtre-Dame des Fontaines, whose interior was painted around 1491 by Giovanni Canavesio. The soldiers in the scenes of the Passion wear remarkably colorful clothing. Saint Peter is being interrogated by a soldier wearing a yellow and black breastplate, a white doublet, red hose, black stockings, yellow shoes, and a sword with a green hilt: a total of five colors. The soldier leading Christ toward Pilate has a red breastplate, black sleeves, a yellow cloak with a green lining, red hose, and black stockings and shoes. Christ and the disciples wear far fewer colors in fewer shades.

In the course of the Middle Ages, people developed a revealing dislike of multicoloredness in clothing, particularly in the form of stripes or checks (see figs. 8, 9, and 10). The gaudy colors we like to think of as exuberant and merrily medieval were used at that time to strike a negative chord. When a painter dressed a figure in hose with one leg red and one leg yellow, he was telling the viewer that this was a dubious character, a deviant, an un-Christian person whose unstable nature was clear for all to see.

Bold color schemes are most apparent in the scenes of the life of Christ depicted in paintings, stained-glass windows, church murals, and books. The torturers and executioners of Jesus, John the Baptist, and all the other saints are often dressed in multicolored apparel with bold designs. These striking figures are counterbalanced by the saints and Christians, clad in simple clothing of one color, who are being goaded, tortured, and executed. In some cases, their blue, red, and whitish cloaks have been snatched from them and lie spread out on the ground—a monochrome indictment of the colorful figures tormenting their white bodies.

A good example of this is the triptych depicting the martyrdom of Saint Hippolytus, painted by Dirk Bouts around 1470 and now in the Groeningemuseum at Bruges. The saint's dark blue cloak is seen in the foreground. Wearing only a white loincloth, he is bound to four horses, who are being spurred on by the executioners to tear him to pieces. The executioners are attired in colorful clothes in overlapping layers. The same contrast is seen on the wings of the triptych. Portrayed on the left are the patrons who commissioned the painting, dressed in dark cloaks and kneeling in prayer; on the right, heathen courtiers in brightly contrasting colors gather round their king.

It is possible that the colorful checkerboard pattern was seen as an expression of extreme disharmony. Perhaps this is why it is so often depicted on floors, which are, after all, trodden upon by feet, the floor representing the impure earth, in which good has been polluted with evil in an unacceptable mixture of garish colors and bold contrasts. It was also assumed that an undesirable alliance between a white man and a black woman would produce a child in a black-and-white checkerboard pattern.

Striped and spotted animals aroused the greatest suspicion, for it was believed that they were too weak to put to use. Karel van Mander again drew on medieval sources—especially the 1583 edition of the fifteenth-century *Blason des couleurs* (Blazon of colors)—when he spiced up his treatise on color with a warning against leopards and tigers. These animals were so splendidly spotted and striped, he opined, that other animals followed them blindly, enticed by the animals' smell as well as their own sense of wonderment, "even though they have to pay for this with their lives." Medieval bestiaries offer very unflattering pictures of spotted animals.

A rich source of such convictions is the Bible. Spotted beasts are singled out in Genesis (30:31–43) as inferior and dubious products of deceit. Van Mander cites the story of the archdeceiver Jacob, who cunningly acquired a large flock of sheep and goats at the expense of his father-in-law, Laban. As wages for seven years of labor—the price of Rachel's hand in marriage—Jacob was promised all the striped, spotted, and speckled animals (traditionally considered the weaker ones) from Laban's enormous flock. Jacob, however, placed partially stripped branches near the drinking troughs of the all-white and all-black animals he also tended and let them mate beside the reflection. They, too, started to produce striped and speckled young. Only the strongest animals were subjected to this method of coupling, the less strong were induced to mate out of sight of the stripped branches and gave birth to uniformly colored offspring. He thus acquired a large and strong—albeit striped and spotted—flock of sheep and goats. The Council of Reims, held in 1148 under the auspices of Pope Eugenius III, complained about the "unseemly diversity of color." Starting in the fourteenth century, this dislike was directed in particular at striped clothing and checkerboard patterns. These clerical campaigns were a reaction to the sudden rise in fashionableness of wild designs among the laity. It henceforth became the height of scandal to be caught wearing such clothes, while bright colors on their own continued to be suspect. Erasmus, in one of his dialogues, puts words of condemnation into the mouth of a stern Franciscan by the name of Koenraad. This friar wants to dress a robber-murderer as humiliatingly as possible by cutting off his shirt above the hips, wrapping him in wolf skins, and dyeing his breeches a bright color.

The persistence of such criticism indicates, however, that clothing fads among the aristocracy—who took little notice of these ecclesiastical outbursts—were difficult to repress. The thirteenth-century hellfire preacher Berthold of Regensburg railed against women who let themselves be carried away by fashionable colors. He noticed that they no longer contented themselves with the infinite variety of colors that God had placed at the disposal of nature—an abundant supply of brown, red, blue, white, green, yellow, and black. No, the latest in female pride involved combining these colors in dots and stripes—red and white, yellow and green—as well as blending them. Surely, this was the umpteenth sign that the end of the world was at hand.

In the Middle Ages, there was a distinct aversion to mixing and blending. Everything that was spotted, striped, or dotted was a reminder of the perversion of the natural elements of Creation, the result of man's reprehensible creative urges, his arrogant attempts to compete with God himself. The punishment for such diabolical hubris manifested itself most visibly in the frequent occurrence of skin diseases (see fig. 11). Animals with bumps or boils, such as toads and dragons, or beasts with spots or stripes, such as hyenas, tigers, and leopards, were similarly damned.

❀

According to the Church, the devil's color campaign had been a success. Eternity was white, divine revelation brilliantly so. On earth, however, the devil had wielded his pernicious palette with abandon. How far he could go depended on humanity itself. Surely God's Creation—nature—had not been polluted for all eternity? Didn't a color such as green denote its very essence?

Such questions fueled the dispute as to what part the devil

played in the application of color. Or were the clerics' arguments actually based on false premises? Wasn't it inconceivable that the devil could have created something as beautiful and perfect as color? At the very least, he had made improper use of it by deluding the human senses. That much was certain. All the pious could do was learn to protect themselves from this most seductive of instruments.

CHAPTER SIX

The Dangers of Yellow, Red, Green, and Blue

Medieval discussions of the amounts, combinations, and gradations of color repeatedly use a disparaging tone to refer to the color yellow. They never actually explain, though, just why yellow was considered so ugly and reprehensible. Medieval sources thought the reason itself undeserving of mention, since they considered all things—colors included—to have intrinsic qualities that needed no justification. They were more interested in interpreting and cataloging than in historical explanations, which they equated with hubris, the same hubris that had caused the fall of the angels under Lucifer's leadership and had made Adam and Eve nibble at the fruit of the tree of the knowledge of good and evil.

Yellow was the color of sorrow, covetousness, hunger, and death, all of which were portrayed on the late-medieval stage as the embodiment of discomfort and disaster. A favorite starting point for such discourse was the apocalyptic "pale" horse in the Book of Revelation (6:8), upon which Death sat. Perhaps yellow also derived its negative connotations from the fact that it was often worn by such outsiders as Jews and Muslims, who were thought to be traitors, just like all non-Christian inhabitants of the Mediterranean region.

By dressing in yellow, therefore, people could express their disapproval—not only at courtly festivities but in real life as well—by means of their color-coded clothes. Hadn't the nobleman Hendrik van Württemberg worn yellow as a way of demonstrating his dislike of the duke of Burgundy? The chronicler Olivier de la Marche reports that in 1474 this knight had ordered his entire retinue to dress in yellow livery to express his loathing as they marched past Charles the Bold. The wearing of certain colors to make a statement during a procession was not at all unusual. In 1411, for example, Parisians demonstrated their allegiance to the duke of Burgundy by wearing blue caps bearing the ducal coat of arms.

Yellow was the color of heathens past and present. It was rarely used in medieval clothing, appearing at most in accessories such as gloves. Very occasionally, the lowest in rank at court—pages and jesters, for instance—dressed in yellow. Not surprisingly, catalogs of virtues and vices such as the *Spiegel der sonden* (Mirror of sins) condemn the color yellow in the severest of terms as being wholly inappropriate for women's clothing. One contributing factor may have been the fact that yellow suffered from the existence of a positive variant in the form of gold. Gold was always advantageous, being representative of the light of the sun and therefore of divine radiance. Little was left to yellow, then, but the negative pole of this color range, which like everything in Creation had two sides: good and evil, earthly and divine. Blue, after all, stood for fidelity but also for duplicity, dissembling, and deceit.

Yellow was the unmistakable sign of an outsider. Jacob van Maerlant tells of a cruel people in the east of India who were big and strong and had "yellow eyes." Elsewhere he quotes an Arabic prophecy that predicts the destruction of Jerusalem and the death of many Christian princes. The conqueror will have black eyes, red cheeks (explained as a sign of aggression in medieval tracts on physiognomy), and powerful limbs, and he will carry a yellow banner. That knightly badge of yellow contained an unwritten message: this man will be a heathen.

The Fourth Lateran Council of 1215 made it compulsory for Jews to wear—preferably over the heart—a yellow identification badge. Alternatively, they could be ordered to wear a pointed yellow hat. The French court followed suit half a century later (in 1269) and decreed that all Jews had to wear a yellow mark of identification. They had to be clearly recognizable in daily life, so that no one would mistake them for Christians, hence a circle the size of the palm of the hand had to be worn on the chest and back. This ordinance was immediately coupled to another one, offering a reward to anyone denouncing Jews in violation of this law. The reward consisted of the outer garments of the offender in question.

Such yellow badges of infamy were also pressed on Muslims, whores, adulterous women, heretics, witches, sorcerers, and even ignoble figures such as executioners. In Lübeck, in 1402, a wandering monk by the name of William, who had been accused of heresy, was sentenced to life imprisonment. Even in the dungeon he was made to wear a penitential yellow cross, which he tore off and trampled underfoot. Yellow, in fact, was used in medieval society to punish all who disgraced themselves in any way. There is evidence that in the Meuse region and Flanders the houses of defaulters and counterfeiters were ordered by the court to be painted yellow.

In literature, the color yellow is used to typify ugliness, untrustworthiness, and betrayal. In the stories of Lancelot, the most valiant knight of King Arthur's Round Table, there is a description of an enemy king who is unbelievably ugly, in itself a sign of bad character. He has a wrinkled forehead, beady eyes like a rat's, a flat nose, long, drooping ears, a cavernously wide mouth, thick lips, and yellow, protruding teeth. Moreover, in the story of the *Vier Heemskinderen* (*The Four Sons of Aymon*), the sorcerer Malegijs manages to change in a twinkling into an old, misshapen beggar. He effects this metamorphosis by drinking a herbal potion that turns him yellow—saffron-colored, to be precise—which sets the tone beautifully for his bogus abasement.

The best evidence for the sinister significance of yellow was provided, however, by the "science" of physiognomy, which teaches that character and disposition can be judged from facial features, such as the color and position of the eyes. Dots around the iris were said to be indicative of wickedness, in accordance with the notion that multicoloredness and wild patterns seldom meant anything good. If such eyes were also brown, however, with the irises ringed with yellow, the person in question was certainly a murderer.

The combination of green and yellow denoted folly, the total madness demonstrated by those who had lost control of their senses and emotions and, like animals, had no power of reason whatsoever (see figs. 12 and 13). Court jesters and all other fools, real or feigned, typically wore green and yellow. The application of this color combination to dubious figures outside the Christian world was also very telling. Exotic, pagan peoples were presented as having features that were the exact opposite of those considered ideal in one's own community. In a way, all those foreigners could also be viewed as fools, since they were completely lacking in Christian powers of reason, which is why the *Blason des couleurs* (Blazon of colors) could assert that "in India, there are people whose entire bodies are yellow and green."

Heraldry also made use of this color scheme, an example being the device of the occasionally hysterical knight Sagremor of the Round Table. This knight had difficulty controlling his emotions and was even subject to fits of rage. One author attributed these fits to Sagremor's tendency to faint from hunger, especially if he hadn't eaten anything by noon. The colors in his coat of arms were, unsurprisingly, green and yellow.

This was also the case with the sensitive Tristan, an indisputable champion among knights owing to his good looks. Unfortunately, though, he was blinded by his passion for Isolde, which turned him into a lovelorn fool. In illuminated manuscripts, he carries a green shield with three golden crowns and wears a green cloak with the same decoration, while his charger's trappings also include a green cloth with golden crowns. Here, the color yellow has doubtless been replaced by gold, in itself positive, to indicate that Tristan's folly is in keeping with the role of tragic hero.

Green and yellow were the colors worn by those pretending to be fools as well as by the truly deranged, who were also required to participate in amusements and ceremonies, both at court and in the city. A miniature in a manuscript dating from 1463 shows Saint

Hubert, who specialized in curing madness and rabies, healing two lunatics. One of them has already had the devil driven out of him and is kneeling, his hands folded in prayer; the other, apparently still in a frenzied state, is being restrained. The point, however, is that these two madmen are dressed identically in green doublets and yellow hose.

The negative connotations of yellow have endured. Throughout the seventeenth and eighteenth centuries, it was common to wear—or suggest that others wear—yellow hose, yellow breeches, or yellow shoes as a sign of jealousy. Moreover, yellow is the traditional color of cowardice, hence references to people with a "yellow streak." And a yellow traffic light, just like a yellow card in soccer, is a warning to be ignored at one's peril.

When yellow meets red, things go from bad to worse, and all the wicked elements in the latter are activated. The result is orange, thought to be very negative indeed (see fig. 14). In medieval times, people with red or carrot-colored hair were considered downright evil, the prime example being the redheaded Judas, the archtraitor who committed the worst betrayal imaginable in exchange for money. In this last respect, he also functioned as the prototype of the Jewish usurer, typically portrayed with red hair. Judas's redness was also evident from his last name—Iscariot—interpreted in German-speaking regions as "is gar rot" ("is very red").

Jacob van Maerlant treats Jews with contempt, calling them a "dirty, unclean, deceitful, ruddy people." In his view, their redheadedness was a direct reference to Jesus' blood, the stain of which they bore for having shed it. Maerlant singles out Esau for special treatment in his narrative adaptation of the Bible: "Listen well, for this tells of Esau, red and hairy. . . . Esau stands for Jews in general, as hairy as they are ruddy, in short, a degenerate people. His red hair is the result of the stain of Christ's blood." An anonymous panegyric on Lord Daniel van der Merwede describes the trouble he encountered when attempting to travel to India after a pilgrimage to the Holy Land. He was thwarted by "the red Jews" who were even worse than ordinary "reds" (in this case, people with scabies).

All the negative implications of redheadedness made the red-haired fox Reynard the most notorious animal in medieval literature. The many tales of his adventures emphasize this trait, by describing him, for example, as "the fierce one with the ruddy beard." Moreover, his youngest son is called Rossel, which means "reddish." A French version of this narrative makes a pointed reference to Judas by having Reynard exchange a conciliatory kiss with a titmouse. When he bends over for the kiss (unavoidable when kissing such a small creature), he resembles Judas betraying Jesus. In any case, his ruddiness has already established his treacherous nature.

Redheadedness was also a characteristic of recalcitrant servants, rebellious sons, perjured brothers, adulterous women, executioners, whores, usurers, money changers, counterfeiters, acrobats, clowns, barber-surgeons, swindling smiths, greedy millers, blood-thirsty butchers, heretics, Jews, Muslims, Bohemians, hypocrites, lepers, the weak and infirm, suicides, beggars, vagabonds, and the destitute. The words used to characterize this motley crew are heathendom, betrayal, usury, and disrepute. It is not surprising, therefore, that warnings were constantly issued against redheads. One scholarly text points with alarm to blushing red faces, which were thought to be indicative of lunacy, aggression, slyness, and betrayal. A fourteenth-century etiquette book cautions against staying in the house of a redhead for the same reasons. Seek lodgings elsewhere, it advises, for such people are impostors and cheats.

We cannot rule out the possibility that redheads were tacitly assumed to be the sinful product of conception during menstruation. Any sexual activity not aimed at procreation was thought to be the work of the devil. Furthermore, it was known that menstrual blood could precipitate disaster. One look from a menstruating woman was enough to cause an infant to break out in spots. A dog who swallowed menstrual blood would instantly turn rabid. Redheaded children, innately crazy and aggressive, must have been conceived at a time when the devil had unleashed his lewd arts of seduction on the unsuspecting. Nature—God's handiwork all the same—took revenge by creating a ruddy mutant that bore witness to such devilry.

The devil himself was also portrayed in red or as a redhead. This is the legacy of ancient and heathen bloodthirstiness, which manifested itself in the color red. In any case, Germanic battle scenes seem to cry out for red. The combatants dyed their hair red before riding out to battle; their war gods, Donar and Wotan, wore red cloaks just like the Roman god of war, Mars. No wonder, then, that Christianity was suspicious of this color, seeing devilry in all things red. Red indicates the presence of Satan, and witches who have made a pact with the devil must be destroyed by red fire. In the Book of Revelation, he who has the power "to take peace from the earth" sits on a red horse (6:4), while the Whore of Babylon is "arrayed in purple and scarlet" and sits on "a scarlet colored beast" (17:3–4). Generally speaking, physical characteristics involving the color red are hardly ever good. In the fifteenth century, a number of people who were banished from Sint Winoksbergen in Flanders for gross misconduct were recorded as having physical characteristics that matched their offensive behavior. There was not only a Gielis with red hair but also a Jacob with a red eye and a Katlijn with two red eyes.

The occasional redheaded hero we encounter among all these scoundrels was apparently put there to prove that everything on earth has its positive side. Just as gradations of yellow include a golden hue, there is also a type of red hair that represents the favorable qualities of red, in the sense of ardor and valor, as exemplified by the Germanic gods. This explains why such biblical heroes as David and Samson can also sport red hair. Nonetheless, the negative connotations of this color, especially when combined with yellow, were generally thought to manifest themselves first and foremost in a red head of hair.

Green was the color most subject to confusion. Primarily the color of earth and nature, green had aroused suspicion from the very beginning. The obvious mutability of nature, as evidenced by the changing of the seasons, meant that all things green were inherently unstable and completely unreliable. This could be interpreted in a more positive sense by emphasizing the fickleness of fortune or fate, which randomly brought good or evil (see fig. 15). This is why gaming tables—whether for cards, gambling, or pool—have been green since the Middle Ages: the outcome on such a surface was never certain (see fig. 16).

Green, moreover, was the first color God used in his Creation, for thus it is written—at least in the Dutch and German versions of the Bible—in Genesis (1:11–12): "On the third day, after dividing the light from the darkness, he sowed the earth with green grass and green plants." No other colors are mentioned in this passage. Thus green was also the color of hope, purity, budding love, and even optimism. The twelfth-century Hildegard of Bingen selects green as the basis for a hymn of praise to the Creator, whose *viriditas* (greenness) she repeatedly applauds. This *Virgo Viridissima*, greenest of maidens, was thought to be obsessed with green and greenness: "No tree grows without the power to become green, no stone lacks green moisture, no being is without this special inner strength, living eternity itself is not without the power to become green."

It was discovered in Hildegard's own day that green surfaces were restful to the eyes, an effect that is still recognized today. The learned William of Auvergne had an explanation for this: green, in his opinion, lay midway between black and white. These two colors forced the eye either to dilate or to constrict. Accordingly, the halfway position of green required the least effort. In the twelfth century, a learned copyist like Baudri of Bourgueil worked only on a writing desk coated with green wax, because it was a comfort to the eyes. The *Tregement der ghesontheyt* (Treatment of health), an authoritative health manual dating from 1514, even recommended regularly strengthening the eyes by staring for a long time into a green basin filled with water. Goethe, too, confidently put this characteristic of green into words: "We look with satisfaction on the simple green of a freshly mown meadow, even though it is only an insignificant patch."

The negative connotations of green persisted, however. Even God's power to produce the green of Creation found detractors. Many a medieval author found the abundance of green in the garden of Eden a bit boring. Unable to resist adding a splash of color, they pointed out that the many fruits and flowers would have provided paradise with colors galore. The most spectacular example of just such a technicolor paradise is certainly Hieronymus Bosch's *Garden of Earthly Delight.*

Color theories may come and go, but they all relegate the color green to second place. Red, blue, and yellow have gradually acquired the status of primary colors. Green is excluded, because it can be obtained by mixing blue and yellow. Piet Mondrian, in search of the definitive autonomy of color, developed a deep dislike of green, which he refused to use in his programmatic work. He even went so far as to avoid looking out the window for fear of being unexpectedly overwhelmed by Mother Nature's aggressive green. Rumor has it that he could not tolerate the presence of real flowers. He permitted only artificial flowers in his studio, and then only after he had painted the green stems and leaves another color.

An antipathy to green can be detected in the work of other painters as well. According to Wassily Kandinsky, the color green was as staid and unoriginal as the bourgeoisie. He was referring not only to the hybrid nature of the color but also to its earthy, grass-roots character, which caused the elite to shy away from it. In this context, it is indeed telling that the use of green is avoided in heraldry. This exclusive device of distinguished families, exhibited in revealing little cachets of arcane colorfulness, shuns green as too common to express anything but the most basic of instincts.

Indeed, from the very beginning green has been associated with humanity's more primary and primitive dealings on earth. For its earliest inhabitants, knowing the color green was a standard part of the survival kit, since varying shades of green supply basic information about the land and its crops—growth, soil conditions, suitability for grazing or cultivation, the presence of water, and the edibility of plants. The earthbound and pastoral character of the color green explains the traditional need for people to distance themselves from nature while at the same time revering it, and this attitude manifests itself in worship of both nature and its Creator.

❀

The color blue has by far the greatest variety of negative connotations and the widest range of possible interpretations. This must have something to do with the extremely positive connotations the color also carries. The more divine and timeless the associations with blue are, the sharper its contrast with its earthly counterparts will be. If the celestial blue of the sky forms a bridge between heaven and earth, Mary—the intermediary par excellence between God and earthly sinners—is almost always clad in blue, a reference to her steadfast and eternal faith, as in the expression "true blue." The earthly counterpart of blue, however, is the transitory world of pretense, deceit, and hypocrisy. And this finds expression in an incredible number of idioms, proverbs, nicknames, and events, many of which still have wide currency.

Earthly blue manifested itself, for example, in the make-believe world of Mardi Gras in the guise of the Blue Barge, which floated on wheels through late-medieval cities, crammed full of merrymakers dressed as ragamuffins, parading as all manner of social outcasts: drunken aristocrats, freeloading monks, lecherous nuns, prodigal sons, lusty housewives, the lame, the blind, and other parasites. Men who had been cuckolded by their wives were forced to wear a hooded cloak of blue; Blue Beguines were whores; Blue Bet was the name of a harlot; blue devotion was pretend piety. And in England, "bluely" used to mean "badly," as in the phrase "to come off bluely."

Nowadays, the color blue is ascribed to things that are hurtful or amoral—"blue murder," for example, and "blue movies"—and a wealth of other meanings that can still be seen in such expressions as "the blues," "blue Monday," and "blue funk." Curious indeed are the expressions created by inventive, if not literary, embroidery on this apparently attractive register. "Bluebeard" is a case in point. And Dutch has a couple of nice terms of abuse— *blauwaard*, or "blue person," and *blauwe schutter*, or "blue marksman"—which are used dismissively to describe impotent lovers. Despite all the help his mistress can give him—described in quite some detail in a sixteenth-century "sottish refrain"—the "blue marksman" not only cannot hit the target but sometimes cannot even find it.

Only a blue devil can mastermind this make-believe world, if he does not succumb, that is, to fits of despondency, or the "blue devils." Devils are at their most fearful in this hue, and so we find them thus portrayed in the paintings of Hieronymus Bosch. Furthermore, the devil's most important allies on earth, the witches, celebrate their Sabbath on Blakulla, meaning "blue hill." Devils in blue are probably also reminiscent of the strong dislike of blue as the color of death and hell in classical antiquity and the early Middle Ages. For Romans, it was the color of barbarians, such as the Celts and the Germanic peoples, who, according to Caesar and Terence, were in the habit of painting their bodies blue in order to scare their enemies to death.

※

To regain the path to eternal life—lost since the Fall—Christians had to learn to read nature like a book. God had filled his Creation with messages that pointed to life after death. The problem was that frail and sickly mankind had lost the ability to decipher these messages, much less take them to heart, especially since the devil— up to his usual tricks—could confound man's senses by setting snares as spurious as they were seductive. Colors are the most hotly debated and misleading of messengers, because the devil can achieve his swiftest and most spectacular successes by using them as allurements. This is why colors can mean almost anything and why they have the power to comfort, to warn, to tempt, and to denote eternity. In other words, every color is ambiguous, but some colors are more ambiguous than others.

CHAPTER SEVEN

The Progress of Decoloration

The medieval world eventually decolored itself. We prefer not to see this but to think instead that medieval men and women possessed an all-purpose palette that enabled them to blot out the grayness of everyday life. We are often envious of the gay and imaginative clothing of the Middle Ages, with its striking, contrasting colors, its daring stripes and checks. And we admire the colorful knights who turned every encounter, serious or festive, into an exhilarating, flag-waving occasion, openly and loudly defying the monotony of existence.

It is remarkable how easily we overlook the medieval view of these color schemes. In those days, it was precisely these colorful, whimsical patterns that expressed alienation, undesirability, and stigmatization. With the same ease, we ignore many other ways in which medieval men and women perceived color, ways less suggestive of ebullient high spirits and more evocative of self-restraint, modesty, and desperate attempts to interpret nature.

Not everyone loved color. Many regarded it as a seductive stunt staged by the devil, who, like a chameleon, could assume every color in the world (see figs. 17 and 18). Anyone who thrilled to the subtle effects produced by a rainbow or stained-glass window was therefore expected to do his utmost to hide the fact. The devil, after all, should not be given the slightest encouragement. Or was it possible that he had already forced his way into our very hearts?

All the stately splendor and wild display of color in the narrow streets of medieval cities eventually prompted those moving in courtly circles to impose severe restrictions on such pomp. The Church led the way, though it struggled throughout the Middle Ages with the dilemma of whether to honor God by offering him priceless treasures or to imitate his son and practice austerity for the sake of humanity's spiritual welfare. Slowly but surely, the anti-color movement prevailed in the world of fashion. Those in courtly circles began to wear black and blue, and, when the Burgundian court also adopted this dress code, the tone was set for lay circles as well. Formal dress has been black ever since (see fig. 19).

The long tradition of decoloration also manifests itself in another trend: our concerted efforts to whitewash (retrospectively) great portions of our past. The large-scale bleaching of classical antiquity, for example, got under way in the eighteenth century and has continued with undiminished vigor to the present day. Consequently, our picture of the ancient world is unquestionably white, as a quick glance at the Asterix and Obelix comics will confirm. We are convinced that the Greeks and Romans walked around in white togas among white marble buildings with white columns.

This is far from the truth, however. Temples and clothes alike were usually brightly colored, so that the classical world must have looked like a cross between Mardi Gras and Disneyland. This does not conform at all to our picture of classical antiquity. In our eyes, that whiteness—an image we believe in so strongly that we feel compelled to re-create it in all our monuments, ancient and modern—is the quintessence of harmony, refinement, and style. If all those authentic fairground colors of yesteryear were to be restored, our whitewashed world would crumble. No matter how much we champion authenticity, no one could be persuaded to paint the Parthenon a nice, bright color. Yet in its heyday this pre-eminent symbol of venerable antiquity was not white but blue.

Who does not shudder at the thought of all those antique marble statues with painted lips, and eyes, hair, and clothing in contrasting colors? It is almost painful to think that the Pont du Gard near Nîmes—that mammoth white aqueduct between the white rocks and green pines of Provence—was once painted fire-engine red. The restoration of such authenticity would strike us as a deliberate attempt to shock the viewer, as misplaced performance art, a blight upon nature, yet another variation on contemporary land art, in which a bridge or landmark is wrapped up, sometimes in startlingly colorful material.

Remarkably, our strong desire to keep the falsification of the past to a minimum is overridden by our even stronger urge to wipe out the colors of the past. In this sense, we exploit the Middle Ages—which were colored in a way that no longer suits us—by taking medieval materials and bending them to our will. This is true in particular of churches. In accordance with the very medieval belief that color was an essential part of God's Creation, medieval builders bestowed color on his earthly dwellings. Painted pillars, stained-glass windows with their kaleidoscopic colors, tapestries, frescoes, altarpieces, painted wallpaper, gold and silver objects inlaid with precious stones, liturgical vestments—to Protestants all these make a church seem more like a circus tent than a quiet house of prayer. There are still a few churches whose interiors recall this once-familiar excess of color, but we are happy to limit ourselves to these infrequent examples (see fig. 20).

Modern art appreciation focuses on medieval statues of stone and wood, which have been preserved by the thousands. Most of these statues were painted in a variety of bright colors, traces of which are sometimes still visible. The vast majority of these statues are now bare stone or highly polished wood, in the latter case dotted with carefully conserved worm holes, which obligingly contribute to the desired effect of authenticity. In fact, we don't want the colors back. A campaign to restore these works to their former glory would meet with little enthusiasm.

In this context, it is enlightening to learn that over the centuries the original colors not only wore off naturally but were also lent a helping hand. Erasmus's personification of Folly was more than happy to do away with color: "I am not so foolish as to ask stone images, painted up in colors; they would but hinder the worship of me, since by the stupid and dull those figures are worshipped instead of the saints themselves." The Church of the Middle Ages has been handed down to us in a faded form, and this is how we want to keep it. Modern taste is not at all ready for a genuine reconstruction of the colors that medieval man found perfectly natural in the house of God. Both the interiors and exteriors of all those wondrous cathedrals, basilicas, parish churches, abbeys, and chapels would seem to us like a fairground house of mirrors, not only because of the color but also because of the overabundance of gleaming bells, shining copper, precious stones, and flickering candles. The often well-preserved interiors of baroque churches give us some idea of what it must have been like, even though the colors do not ring true. Their white or pastel hues would have to be converted into bright, deep colors in clashing combinations that would offend our modern sensibilities.

A few well-preserved church interiors still display their authentic colors: the previously mentioned chapel near La Brigue, for example, and the monumental fortress church of Albi. Visitors to these churches cannot help being startled when they cross the threshold. The Reformation ushered in an era of restraint, and ever since then we have expected churches to be places of meditation and prayer. No distractions are permitted, and certainly no display of colors evincing things more quotidian than eternal.

This attitude also existed in the Middle Ages. It did not result in the decoloring of the churches, however, despite the example set by more than one Cistercian abbey. The inclination to honor God by decorating everything as richly as possible proved to be irrepressible. Abbot Suger of Cluny was the embodiment of that ideal. The elation he felt at the colorful splendor he thought appropriate to divine worship is still infectious. In Suger's view, light and color had to be so well attuned that their harmonies transcended even those of a church's architecture. All available means were deployed to transform the church into a temple of color, brought to life by light:

painted windows, floors, walls, pillars, vaults, woodwork, doors, wallpaper, furniture, valuable objects, liturgical vestments, paintings, statues, enamel, wrought ironwork, and precious stones.

❀

Suger's views did not prevail: the medieval world was ultimately stripped of its color. The strict regulations imposed in the late Middle Ages paved the way for the Reformation's dominant color scheme of black, white, and gray, which sounded the death knell for these colors as colors. Thus far, attempts to revive the medieval wealth of color have not been successful. The baroque period and the age of romanticism gave way to neoclassicism and all the other "neo" styles, with their severe black-and-white color schemes.

The rise of pastel shades in the twentieth century did not prove to be a roundabout route to the restoration of exuberant colors. Mass production and large-scale consumerism have made deep aristocratic colors such as violet and purple seem vulgar, only fit now for jogging suits and leisure wear. The decline of purple is a good example of the disinclination to embrace color. In classical antiquity, this dyestuff was obtained from rare snails, making it so exclusive that by the fourth century only the emperor was allowed to wear purple garments. Its exclusivity continued into the Middle Ages. The thirteenth-century poet Jacob van Maerlant confirmed this, although he believed that purple dye was obtained from elephants' blood. It was not until the beginning of the twentieth century that it finally became possible to manufacture a synthetic purple dye, but by then no one was interested in the color. Thus the mass production of colors, which put them within reach of everyone, has actually led to decoloration.

This development inevitably began with industrialization. In 1877 Charles de Coster, author of a French adaptation of *Thyl Ulenspiegel* in which the hero figures as a Marxist, a militant Fleming, a revolutionary, and a Freemason, took a trip through the Low Countries. Surprised at the democratization of color—seen in the great variety of hues worn by people in the street—he wrote down his impressions. In Amsterdam, he found himself among thick crowds "in which there were many bright spots of lilac and pink, the favorite colors of domestic servants in all of Holland." In the shops, he saw scarves and fabrics "in all manner of dazzling colors. People buy everything they need here." It appears to have dawned on him for the first time that once-exalted colors like lilac no longer stood for wealth and luxury and were certainly no longer capable of lending status to the wearer.

In our day, this has prompted the triumphal reentry of black, white, and gray, the colors most often chosen by the *nouveaux cultivés* for their automobiles, interiors, and formal attire. It now looks less likely than ever that an era as thoroughly colorful as the Middle Ages will ever make a comeback. Color has gradually been relegated to a world of fleeting emotions, impossible to pin down. Within the context of a rational life, color can therefore be seen as an irrational infringement on civilized life. As such, color appears increasingly to represent the irrepressible outpourings of a rebellious, carnivalesque world—a reminder that reason and self-denial cannot continue to exist without being periodically rejected. At the same time, however, these periods of rejection emphasize, by virtue of their brevity and transience, the upsurge and implacable progress of decoloration. Surely it is no coincidence that writers and painters set the tone for these occasional lapses into deliberate disorder.

We are all familiar with the revolt of the impressionists against the gray and dusky tones that made works of art seem as though they had been doused with brown sauce. At Claude Monet's funeral, his friend Clemenceau snatched the black shroud from his coffin and replaced it with a colorful curtain that he had ripped from a nearby window. After all, black was an insult to the impressionists, who had banned it from their palette. The success of their revolution has made it difficult for us to realize that for a long time painting had been dominated by dark colors, particularly shades of brown. Reacting to this, Theo van Gogh—with his thorough knowledge of the art trade—wrote on October 22, 1889, to his brother Vincent: "In Belgium, they are more accustomed to colorful painting; the exhibition of the *Vingtistes* did some good in this respect; nonetheless, no one is buying any of it." And Vincent declared more than once in his letters to Theo that the painter of the future would be a colorist.

The impressionists' brilliant barrage doubtless sparked off a more general appreciation of color in twentieth-century society. This revolt, however, did nothing at all to halt the advance of decoloration. Instead, there was a revealing rise in the popularity of pastel shades—colors that dare not speak their name—which seemed to offer the elite a kind of compromise between the colors esteemed in their circles—black, blue, gray, and white—and the bright colors of the masses. These hypocritical hues began to color interiors and consumer products as fashionable as they were costly, turning up in kitchens, bathrooms, and bedrooms in the form of sheets, towels, underwear, and nightclothes. Even automobiles felt the onslaught of pastel colors. The elite, however, eventually distanced themselves from these colors as well. Once pastels had been imitated and democratized, they no longer served as a mark of distinction. The cultured and well-to-do now take refuge, as they always have, in the familiar black-and-white color scheme.

The promotion of color still strikes a chord of defiance in its struggle against the apparent hegemony of dark and light. Mondrian tried to rationalize color by removing it from the realm of emotion, hoping in this way to link up with a world of learning and culture in which color could once again represent the quintessence of existence. To this end, it was necessary not only to tame colors but also to reduce them to their basic form: "The principle is that color should be free from individuals as well as from individual emotions and should express only the quiet perception of the universe."

Vincent van Gogh also wrestled with the black-and-white scheme, trying initially to turn the color revolution into a generally acknowledged success by pointedly restoring black and white to their rightful place among the colors. Wasn't the contrast between black and white just as strong as that between green and red, for example? The literature of this time bears witness to the writers' eagerness to take part in the painters' revolution. Their attempt to color the world of words was decidedly forced, however, enhancing rather than negating the impression that colors represent added value of a fleeting nature, dependent on the arbitrary impression of random passers-by. The nineteenth-century Dutch poet Willem Hofdijk provides the perfect example:

> When white beeches brown are turning
> And the silver birch is gold
> And the trembling poplars, yellowing,
> Ash trees wrapped in misty blue,
> Reddish plumes do crown the reeds
> And berries of a ruby hue
> Are mirrored in the brownish stream . . .

A similar color insurgency occurred in the 1960s and 1970s. Disguised at first as a youthful protest, the new counterculture soon dictated bright colors in clothing, consumer goods, and interiors. It was not long before businessmen were wearing flowery ties, and homeowners were painting their living rooms in bold, contrasting colors or such supposedly harmonious combinations as orange and yellow. Seldom has color so obviously served as a vehicle of social protest, following as it did in the wake of the revolt against "the system" and the authority wielded by the older generation— the champions of the civilized regime of dark hues. The rebellion was short-lived, however, and so, too, was the once trend-setting hegemony of color among the cultured elite.

❀

Apart from such dialectic upheavals, the tendency is to relegate color to a counterrealm existing outside the set pattern of everyday life: vacations, for example, and art in all its forms. Even then, colors often yield to black and white, for these timeless hues continue to set the tone for elegant dinners, concerts, first nights at the opera, weddings, and funerals.

The nineteenth century, in particular, and to some extent the twentieth managed to get along perfectly well without color. Typography, photography, and prints in everyday circulation were chiefly black and white, whereas distinction of manner presented itself in black or gray. At the end of the nineteenth century, the new field of experimental psychology was at pains to prove that a love of primary colors was displayed not just by young children and primitive peoples but also by civilized adults in one's own society. This notion—that a fascination with color was natural in primitive peoples—had a long tradition. In the Middle Ages, it was believed that tribal peoples not yet touched by Christianity took an irrational delight in bright colors. The fourteenth-century globetrotter Sir John Mandeville—whose travels took place largely in his imagination—maintained that the inhabitants of an island in the South Seas "cared nothing for gold, silver, or other worldly goods." This was very positive from a Christian point of view, as it was completely in keeping with the conviction that there were peoples who still lived in a state of paradisiacal innocence. Unfortunately, Mandeville added, their unspoiled minds had been filled with idle color worship. He went on to say that they cared "only for one precious stone which has sixty colors. It is called traconite after the country. They love this stone very much indeed, even though they do not know its properties; they desire it simply for its beauty." Ignorant of the mystical powers of this stone, which were undisputed in the Christian world, they loved it for its color alone. Such aesthetic considerations were anathema to Mandeville, if only because they were so superficial. But what could one expect from such simple souls?

Perhaps colors are beginning more and more to represent a nostalgia for lost happiness, the right we once had—and think we still have—to a better life in the hereafter. Seen in this light, colors stand for a lost paradise that once dazzled with brilliance. We seek this paradise beyond the gray drabness of a daily life that, in the guise of culture, is pushing us further and further away from earthly fulfillment and is thus decoloring—imperceptibly yet inexorably—our very existence. And on our quest for that lost garden of color, we are constantly running up against new color theories, dialectic rebellions taking the form of everything from venturesome vacations to full-blown revolutions, including the unmitigated enthusiasm of the color-crazed madness to which Van Gogh treated us more convincingly than any other artist has ever done.

That color should remain so elusive is perhaps gratifying, certainly now that it has increasingly come to inhabit that counter-world whose existence makes the ever more colorless life of everyday somehow bearable. Parties, art, and culture now belong to the realm of color excess, whereas the tenor of official life is determined by black, white, gray, and an obligingly dark blue. Thus colors have been cast in the role of rewards, of comforts, serving to bandage the wounds inflicted by humanity's fall from grace. This is very much the way French peasants saw color in the twelfth century, when a young man would plunge himself into lifelong debt in order to present his bride with a scarlet cloak. This was the colorful answer to a life of suffering.

(p. 15)

DIT IS VAN •VI• VAERWEN ENDE •XII• OUTHEYDEN DEEN METTEN
ANDEREN BEDIEDT

Ses varuwen sijn op erden,
Die God op erden liet ghewerden,
Met siner wonnentlike goede,
Om dat die minsche met vrien moede
Sinen God soude leeren
Daer in dancken ende eren.

(p. 16)
Wi zijn al mal, 't is ons gheval;
Wi willen't ooc wel weten!
In't aertsche dal maecken wi gheschal,
Ons wijsheyt is versleten.
Wi en kennen groen, wit, swart noch root;
Waer vint men meerder dwasen?
Onse sotheyt is so groot,
Si blijft ons bi tot in der doot;
We en konnen niet dan rasen!

(p. 26)
Ze kleurt en verft en smeedt en snijdt
ridders, gewapend tot de strijd

op hun strijdrossen, vurig-wilde,
met blauw, geel, groene wapenschilden,
of met een andre kleur op 't schild,
als u dat nog veel bonter wilt.

(p. 29)
Li uns se vest pour li de vert,
L'autre de bleu, l'autre de blanc,
L'autre s'en vest vermeil com sanc,
Et cilz qui plus la veult avoir
Pour son grant dueil s'en vest de noir.

(p. 30)
Au bleu vestir ne tient mie le fait,
N'à devises porter, d'amer sa dame,
Mais au servir de loyal cuer parfait
Elle sans plus, et la garder de blasme
 . . . Là gist l'amour, non pas au bleu porter,
Mais puet estre que plusieurs le meffait
De faulseté cuident couvrir soubz lame
Par bleu porter . . .

(p. 34)
Een ordine hevet mijn herte up heven,
Dats zwart, dat heift soe an ghedaen.
Een graeu doet soe daer binnen cleven.
Dit heift zoe ervelic ontfaen.
Heo slasi dan haer van zorghen dwaen?
Want zwart es rauwe ende graeu arbeit.
Dus heift zoe lust no vroylicheit.

(p. 96)
Als de blanke beuken bruinen
En de zilvren berk staat goud
En de klaterpopels gelen,
Wazig blauw omwentelt de essen,
Rosse pluimen toppen 't riet
En de rode sporkenbessen
Spieglen in den bruinen vliet . . .

All translations are mine unless otherwise specified.—Trans.

Introduction

John Gage, *Colour and Culture* (1994) is easy to use, beautifully illustrated, and contains a large bibliography; Michel Pastoureau's studies are also a good point of departure: *Figures et couleurs* (1986), *Couleurs, images, symboles* (1989a), *Jésus chez la teinturier* (1997). For a general introduction to the subject, see also C. A. Beerli, *Poétique et société des couleurs* (1993); T. Lamb and J. Bourriau, eds., *Colour: Art and Science* (1995); M. Bruns, *Das Rätsel Farbe* (1997). J. Huizinga provides a stimulating introduction to the subject in *The Waning of the Middle Ages* (1924), in chap. 20, "The Aesthetic Sentiment." Many writers still adopt Huizinga's ideas about color. R. van Uytven published a detailed overview of the subject in the *Tijdschrift voor geschiedenis* 97 (1984): 447–69, which is continued in *De zinnelijke Middeleeuwen* (1998), 84-119. G. C. den Boer offers interesting insights in his thesis (supervised by F. P. van Oostrom) submitted to Leiden University: *Inventariserend onderzoek naar het kleurgebruik in Middelnederlandse teksten* (1985). New views are to be found in P. Dronke, *The Medieval Poet and His World* (1984), 55–03. Detailed studies written by a variety of authors are published in *Les couleurs au moyen âge* (1988). Chr. Meier talks about the compilation of a medieval color catalog in *Frühmittelalterliche Studien* 21 (1987): 390–478, and gives an example based on the color red. Aristotle's remarks appear in "Aristoteles," in *Over kleuren*, ed. R. Ferwerda (2001), 74 and 84; cf. Bruns 1997, 15–16. Vincent van Gogh in *Brieven* (1990), 3:1308. On the devil: H. Pleij, "Duivels in de Middelnederlandse literatuur," in *Duivelsbeelden*, ed. G. Rooijakkers, L. Dresen-Coenders, and M. Geerdes (1994), 89–106. The first Bernard of Clairvaux quotation is from M. Pastoureau, "L'église et la couleur des origines à la réforme," *Bibliothèque de l'École des Chartes* 147 (1989b): 208. On the Cistercians and color, see G. Duby, *Bernard van Clairvaux en de Cisterciënzer kunst* (1989), esp. 126 for the quotation. Information on modern color appreciation in Pastoureau 1989a, 10–14; regarding the rise of the color blue, see ibid., 23–24, 35–38; idem 1997, 101–14. Examples of recipes for dyes are in W. L. Braekman, *Middelnederlandse verfrecepten* (1986).

1. Medieval Notions of Color

The color of goose dung in *Een warachtig seer vreemde ende wonderlijcke gheschiedenisse . . . int lant van Mijssen* (1542), fol. [A]2 recto. Overviews of various theories are in J. Mac Lean in *Scientiarum Historia* 7 (1965): 213–18; Dronke 1984; and the contributions by Huë and Salvat to the volume *Les couleurs au moyen âge* (1988). Bartholomaeus Anglicus summarizes many of these notions in vol. 19 of *De proprietatibus rerum* (On the properties of things) (1485). On etymologies, see also M. Pastoureau 1989b, 206–7 (Isidore of Seville is quoted on 207); idem 1997, 34–35; cf. *Middelnederlandsch Woordenboek* s.v. "couleur." Pastoureau, L'église, 1989, p. 207. The *exemplum* of the black baby is in the *Blason des couleurs* (1860), 71–72; the others are in K. van Mander, *Den grondt der edel vry schilderconst* (1973), 270 and 267. Hugo of St. Victor is quoted in Meier 1987, 390–91. For definitions in general, see also the *Lexikon des Mittelalters* and the *Handwörterbuch des deutschen Aberglaubens*, both under "Farbe"; see also Pastoureau 1997, passim. Quotations taken from *Dat batement van recepten* (1990), nos. 42 and 102; *De Bouc vanden Ambachten* (1931), 31, 45; *Twee zestiende-eeuwse spelen van de hel* (1934), B 597–600, B 469–70. The Haarlem oath is in J. Huizinga, *Rechtsbronnen der stad Haarlem* (1911), 457–58; to compare with Leiden, see N. W. Posthumus, *De geschiedenis van de Leidse lakenindustrie* (1908–39), 1:50–51, 68–69. On the preparation of costly pigments, see Pastoureau 1997, passim; for purple, see Gage 1994, 258; J. van Maerlant, *Der naturen bloeme* (1878), vol. 2, lines 1424–25; on the extraction of scarlet, see idem, vol. 5, lines 779–90. Regarding earth and nature as a sign system, see F. Ohly in *Schriften zur mittelalterliche Bedeutungsforschung* (1977), esp. 32–92 on the use of color. "Een moy sprake van sesterhande verwe" was published by K. de Flou and J. Gaillard, *Beschrijving van Middelnederlandsche handschriften in Engeland*,(1895–97), no. 60. On liturgical colors, see H. Sachs, *Erklärendes Wörterbuch zur christlichen Kunst* (1973), 130–32. The "sottish refrain" is in *Een schoon Liedekens-Boeck* (1968), no. 169. Quotations taken from van Maerlant and von der Vogelweide are to be found in van Uytven 1984, 451–52. On the dyeing industry, in both the cities and the countryside, see Pastoureau 1989, esp. 24 and 29; idem 1997; and *Lexikon des Mittelalters* under "Farbe." For more on colors and clothing, see Chr. de Merindol in *Recherches sur l'économie de la France médiévale* (1989), 221–42; T. Ruiz in *Annales ESC* 46 (1991): 521–46.

2. Colors in Daily Life

Bertran de Born is cited in Duby 1989, 22. The colorful shields occur in van Uytven 1998, 87. Quotation from *Walewein* (1983), 166, 169. Froissart is cited in J. Huizinga, *Herfsttij der Middeleeuwen* (1997), 298; Ruusbroec is quoted from *Werken* (1932), 4:147–48. On urban partisanship and colors, see C. de Haan and J. Oosterman, *Is Brugge groot?* (1996), 9–10; cf. R. Stein, *Politiek en historiografie* (1994), 222; O. Delepierre, in *Annales de la Société d'Emulation de Bruges*, 1842: 253–55. Regarding heralds and their work, see W. van Anrooij, *Spiegel van ridderschap* (1990). Poem translated from the Dutch version in the *Roman van de roos*, translated from the French by E. van Altena (1991), lines 16009–14 (not in the Middle Dutch version). On Rabelais, see M. A. Screech in *Mélanges d'histoire du XVIe siècle offerts à H. Meylan* (1970), 65–80; Gage 1994, 89. The quotations from Rabelais's *Gargantua and Pantagruel* are taken from the translation by Burton Raffel (1990), 26–27. Clothes, color, and meanings in de Merindol (1989). "Van suveren Cledren te dragen alle vrouwen" is in *Vaderlandsch Museum* 1 (1855): 350–52; "De ghelasen sale" is in *Klein kapitaal uit het handschrift–Van Hulthem* (1992), 57–69; Potter is discussed in A. M. J. van Buuren, *Der minnen loep* (1979), 138–54; Deschamps in Huizinga 1997, 299. For the German material, see T. Brandis, *Minnereden* (1968), 141–46; I. Glier, *Artes amandi* (1971), 106–9; W. Gloth, *Das Spiel von den sieben Farben* (1902). Christine de Pisan is in Huizinga 1997, 299. On the clothing worn by a knight at his investiture, see Gage 1994, 84. For colors and moods at the court of René of Anjou, see van Uytven 1984, 448. On the anticolor movements in the Church: Duby 1989; Pastoureau 1989a, 32–39; Pastoureau 1989b; Gage 1994, 84. The examples concerning Joinville and Louis IX are in A. Borst, *Lebensformen im Mittelalter* (1973), 195–98. Quotation taken from S. Brant, *Das Narrenschiff* (1966), chap. 82. The song comes from the Gruuthuse manuscript: *Liederen* (1966), no. 36. On Charles V, see Bruns 1997, 224; the black worn by Philip the Good is found in Pastoureau 1997, 140; regarding black in general, see Gage in Lamb and Bourriau 1995, 188–89. T. B. Husband, in *The Luminous Image* (1995), describes this turning point in terms of the colors displayed by stained-glass windows.

3. Beautiful Colors for Mere Enjoyment?

P. Brinkman treats *Het geheim van Van Eyck* (1993). Medieval notions of nature are discussed by C. J. Glacken, *Traces of the Rhodian Shore* (1967); D. Pearsall, *Landscapes and Seasons of the Medieval World* (1973); G. Duby, *De middeleeuwse liefde* (1990), esp. 79–112; A. Verrycken, *De middeleeuwse wereldverkenning* (1990); W. Cahn in *Yale French Studies*, 1991 (special issue): 11–24. On heresy and dreamworlds, see N. Cohn, *The Pursuit of the Millennium* (1984); H. Pleij, *Dreaming of Cockaigne* (2001), 301–34. Petrarch's letter is to be found in *De top van de Ventoux* (1990), 7–17. The quotation was taken from *Dat boeck van den pelgherym* (1486); the meadows in Bartholomaeus Anglicus are cited in Cahn 1991, 24; Hugo of St. Victor is in Dronke 1984, 84; the pilgrim's account is in C. Deluz in *Les couleurs au moyen âge* (1988), 67. Ottonian book illumination is discussed in H. Jantzen, *Middeleeuwse kunst in overgang* (1961), 138–42; the representation of Jesus' entry on the donkey in E. Pirani, *Romanische Miniaturen* (1974), fig. 6; for the miniature of God on his throne, see the guide to the Westfälisches Landesmuseum Münster (1981), 53. For color as a mnemonic device, see M. Carruthers, *The Book of Memory* (1994), 9, 133–34, 282.

4. The Most Beautiful Colors Adorn the Woman

Examples of ideals of feminine beauty in the older literature are given by G. Degroote in *Dietsche Warande en Belfort* (1956), 202–14. For the meanings of green, brown, and black, see Pastoureau 1989a, 31, 33–34, 49. Regarding the aversion to blue in classical antiquity, see Pastoureau 1997, 97. Quotations and paraphrases taken from A. de Roovere, *Gedichten* (1955), 397–99; A. Bijns, *'t Is al vrouwenwerk* (1987), 23, 26, and afterword; J. van Maerlant, *Strophische gedichten* (1918), 129–31, lines 313–90; Matthew of Vendôme, *The Art of Versification* (1980), 43. Bartholomaeus Anglicus, *Van den proprieteyten der dinghen* (1485), chap. 19. Halewijn is discussed in G. Komrij, *De Nederlandse poëzie van de 12de tot en met de 16de eeuw in duizend en enige gedichten* (1994), 466–71; *Dmeisken in Middelnederlandse boerden* (1957), 22–24; A. Bijns, in *Leuvensche bijdragen* 4 (1902): 242; scattered references are in Pastoureau 1997, 159–60; J. van Maerlant, *Historie van Troyen* (1889), vol. 1, lines 6801–68; *Boeck vander destructien van jherusalem* (1482), fol. [l7] verso; *Roman van Lancelot* (1846–49), lines 11812–14, cf. line 13331; *Der Vrouwen Natuere ende Complexie, ca. 1538* (facsimile edition 1980), fol. [D1] recto; H. van Aken, *Die rose* (1878), lines 797–806; van Mander (1973), 273. On self-mutilation, see, for instance, S. Raue, *Een nauwsluitend keurs* (1996), 214–18. For Polyxena, J. van Maerlant, *Historie van Troyen* (1889), vol. 1, lines 7031–66. Regarding the white throat and the red wine, see van Uytven 1998, 110. The mistrust of things new and original is discussed in H. Pleij in *Hoort wonder! Opstellen voor W. P. Gerritsen* (2000), 121–26. Dronke 1984, 60–63, refers to the place in the Celtic text; cf. M. Draak and F. de Jong, *Van helden, elfen en dichters* (1979), 148–49.

5. The Devil's Pernicious Palette

Quotation from Gregory in Pastoureau 1989b, 206, as well as more general information about the Church's fight against colors. Ideas about colors in the *Blason des couleurs*, 69–73. The examples from Hermas's work are found in Dronke 1984, 64–66. On white, see Bruns 1997, 186–214; E. de Bruyn, *De vergeten beeldentaal van Jheronimus Bosch* (2001), 75–76. On Bernard of Clairvaux, see Bruns 1997, 21; *Utopia* is in Gage 1994, 69. Hugo of Folieto is cited in Ohly 1977, 79; Bernard of Clairvaux in Duby 1989, 125. The Fourth Lateran Council is quoted in Pastoureau 1989b, 227. On the Antwerp Beguines, see W. A. Olyslager, *750 jaar Antwerpse begijnen* (1990), 185. On changing one's color, see *Rinclus* (1893), lines 1005–22; *Die buskenblaser* in *Handschrift-Van Hulthem* (1999), vol. 2, lines 1127–36; *His-*

torie van Jason, thesis submitted to Amsterdam University (1980), 19. The detestable tendency of women to paint their faces is invariably discussed in such moralizing works as *Die spiegel der sonden* (1900), vol. 5, chaps. 31–33; cf. *Rinclus*, lines 1179–1214; Ruusbroec 1932, 3:118–19; Boendale in F.-A. Snellaert, *Nederlandsche gedichten uit de veertiende eeuw* (1869), 276–79, lines 39–56; 209–13, lines 2154, 2194–99; van Maerlant 1918, vol. 2, lines 20–21. The quotations from *The Romance of the Rose* were taken from the translation by Frances Horgan (1994), 169–171. Seuse is cited in Dronke 1984, 72; Mary's lament at the foot of the cross is found in *Vanden levene Ons Heren* (1968), lines 3433–3514. Bartholomaeus Anglicus (1485), fol. Y4 recto, discusses the mutability of colors; cf. van Maerlant, *Der naturen bloeme* (1878), vol. 8, lines 523–28. Polychromy is treated in Pastoureau 1989b, 227; idem 1997, 156–63; de Merindol 1989, 210–11; the bastard child in Pastoureau 1989a, 18. See van Mander 1973, 270, on striped animals. The Council of Reims is cited in Pastoureau 1989b, 227. See Erasmus, *Tweede twaalftal samenspraken* (1913), 89. Berthold of Regensburg is cited in A. L. A. Roessingh, *De vrouw bij de Dietsche moralisten* (1914), 60; cf. in general *Geschiedenis van de vrouw*, edited by G. Duby, vol. 2 (1991), 139–60. For the opposition to mixing colors, see Pastoureau 1997, 58–59.

6. The Dangers of Yellow, Red, Green, and Blue

On the negative assessment of yellow, see van Uytven 1984, 448–51; Pastoureau 1989a, 49–51, 70–72; Bruns 1997, 85. Württemberg is in Huizinga 1997, 301; cf. Pastoureau 1997, 153; van Uytven 1998, 89. See *Spiegel* (1900), vol. 5, chap. 32, on yellow in women's clothing. Van Maerlant's remarks occur in the *Spiegel historiael* (1857–63), part 1, book 1, chap. 31, lines 51–53; part 4, book 7, chap. 36, lines 11–16. Regarding the yellow badges worn by Jews, see also Pastoureau 1997, 137–38; cf. R. E. Lerner, *The Heresy of the Free Spirit* (1972), 149–51, on the heretic William of Lübeck. Quotations are from *Lancelot* (1846–49), vol. 3, chap. 42, lines 18292–18301; *Vier Heemskinderen* (1931), 155; *Heimlicheit der heimlicheden*, in N. de Pauw, *Middelnederlandsche gedichten en fragmenten* (1893), 130, lines 313–20. See *Blason des couleurs*, 120–21, on the yellow-green peoples of India. Sagremor and Tristan are discussed in Pastoureau 1986, 24–28; cf. F. P. van Oostrom, *Lantsloot vander Haghedochte* (1981), 154–56; the Vienna *Tristan* manuscript is described in D. Thoss, *Tristan and Isolde* (1978) and the Saint

Hubert miniature in H. H. Beek, *Waanzin in de Middeleeuwen* (1969), vol. 12. The negative implications of red are covered in W. Kuiper in *Opstellen aangeboden aan F. Lulofs* (1980), 130–39; R. Bellon in *Les couleurs au moyen âge* (1988), 15–28; van Uytven 1984, 461–63. Regarding Judas, see Pastoureau 1989a, 69–79; R. Mellinkoff in *Journal of Jewish Art* 9 (1982): 31–46. The quotations from van Maerlant, physiognomy, and the etiquette book are from Kuiper 1980, 134–35; cf. van Maerlant, *Rijmbijbel*, ed. Gysseling, in *Corpus* (1983), lines 2185–93 and 2211–14. Van der Merwede's panegyric is in J. Smits, *Beschrijving der stad Dordrecht* (1844), 149–57, esp. line 55. See Bellon 1988, 21, on Reynard's resemblance to Judas; the quotation is taken from the English translation (*Reynard the Fox*) by Adriaan J. Barnouw (1967), line 60. The theory about redheadedness as punishment for conception during menstruation is from Kuiper 1980, 136. For red, yellow, and carrot-colored in general, see also Pastoureau 1997, 147–51. On red in non-Christian cultures, see Bruns 1997, 51–53; on the outcasts, van Uytven (1998), 91. On green in general, see Bruns 1997, 108–35; Pastoureau 1997, 70–78. Quotations from Hildegard of Bingen in Bruns 1997, 126, 133–34. Baudri's green washbasin is described in van Uytven 1998, 92. See *Tregement der ghesontheyt* (1514), fol. d1 verso, column b. Goethe is cited in Bruns 1997, 108. On the modern antipathy to green, see Gage 1994, 258; Bruns 1997, 129. On blue in general, see Bruns 1997, 136–66; Pastoureau 1997, 101–14. The Blue Barge is discussed in H. Pleij, *Het Gilde van de Blauwe Schuit* (1983). Proverbs, expressions, and other "blue" usages in Dutch are to be found in the *Middelnederlandsch Woordenboek* and the *Woordenboek der Nederlandse Taal;* "blue" usages in English can be found in the *Oxford English Dictionary*; all three dictionaries are available on CD-ROM. See also J. Cornelissen in *Ons Volksleven* 7 (1895): 51–54, with a great many references to blue (*blauw*); J. J. Mak, *Rhetoricaal glossarium* (1959), for words and expressions derived from *blauw*; J. Sartorius, *Adagiorum chiliades tres* (1561), part 2, chap. 4, no. 34, chap. 5, no. 85, chap. 9, no. 40. E. de Bruyn, *De vergeten beeldentaal van Jheronimus Bosch* (2001), 424–25, gives many instances of *blauw* in the literature. See W. Jappe Alberts, *De middeleeuwse stad* (1968), 99, for the name Blue Bet; J. van Doesborch, *Refreinenbundel* (1940), no. 151, on impotence; cf. Komrij 1994, 662–65, with a *blauwe schutter*; for blue devils in Dutch literature, see de Bruyn 2001, 83–85; *Evangelie van den Spinrocken* (1992), 21. The "blue hill" (*blauwe heuvel*) is mentioned in P. Spierenburg, *De verbroken betovering* (1998), 150.

7. The Progress of Decoloration

The bright colors in churches are discussed in Duby 1989; Pastoureau 1989a, 61–63; Pastoureau 1989b, 215. On black in the world of fashion, see Gage in Lamb 1995, 188–89. The coloredness of classical antiquity is treated in Lamb 1995, 7; "Aristoteles," 11–12. Quotation taken from Erasmus, *The Praise of Folly*, trans. Hoyt Hopewell Hudson (1969), 67. Regarding colored buildings in the Middle Ages, see H. Hofrichter, ed., *Putz und Farbigkeit am mittelalterlichen Bauten* (1993); van Uytven 1998, 95. On purple, see Gage 1994, 25; Bruns 1997, 177–84. Fashionable colors are discussed in Charles de Coster, *Bloedzuigers* (1964), 10–11. Regarding the impressionists and Clemenceau, see Bruns 1997, 237. For the letter, see van Gogh, *Brieven* (1990), vol. 4; cf. K. Badt, *Die Farbenlehre Van Goghs* (1981), 66. Quotation from Mondrian taken from Bruns 1997, 128–29. Quotations from Hofdijk taken from G. Brom, *Schilderkunst en literatuur in de 19e eeuw* (1959), 22. See *The Travels of Sir John Mandeville*, trans. C. W. R. D. Moseley (1983), 134. The peasants' scarlet cloak is mentioned in Duby 1989, 16.

cities: colorful places, 21, 90; distrust of colorful clothing, 32; urban aristocracy, 6

class: artisans, 19–20; bourgeoisie, 25; bright colors and, 33; clothing and, 24–25, 27; color and, 6, 20–21, 32–34; lower middle class, 20–21; skin color, 53–54; urban aristocracy, 6; wealth, 20, 94; workers, 20–21. *See also* aristocrats; clergy; elite groups; knights; nouveaux riches; peasants

Clemenceau, Georges, 94

clergy: bishops, 32; cardinals, 32; clothing, 25; monks, 32; symbol of mendicancy, 32; use of color, 20. *See also* religious orders

clothing: anticolor sentiments, 32, 67–68, 90; aristocrats, 25, 75; blue, 30–31; bourgeoisie, 25; character and color of, 70–75; checks, 72–73, 74; of Christians, 73; class and, 24–25, 27; clergy, 25; colorful, 6; contrasting colors, 5, 89, 90–91; dark colors and, 34; drab colors, 5, 6, 25; fashionableness of wild designs, 74; formal dress, 90, fig. *19*; green, 67; headscarves, 66, 68; jesters, 78; jogging suits, 93; knights, 23, 31; leisure wear, 93; lovers, 28, 29–30; lower middle class, 20–21; Mary, 86; multicoloredness, 72–73, fig. *8*, fig. *9*, fig. *10*; nouveaux riches, 6, 33; pages (at court), 78; peasants, 33; political expression, 77–78; pride expressed in, 68; princes, 6; Rabelais on, 27; red, 67, 83; rules for, 24; saints', 71, 73; soldiers', 72;

stripes, 72–73, 74, 75, fig. *10*; symbolism of, 24–25, 30, 31; undyed cloth, 32; wolf in sheep's, 71; women's, 6, 25, 68; workers, 20–21; yellow, 67, 78

coats of arms: colorfulness of, 85; diplomats', 25; of the duke of Burgundy, 78; heralds' descriptions of, 26; of knights in armor, 26; portrayed by artists, 39; Sagremor's, 80; on warships, 24

Cologne, 46

color: aestheticizing use of, 46–47; age groups and, 6; ambiguity of, 87–88; as an accessory, 2; beauty and, 47; bright colors, 6, 7, 33, 37, 95, 97; brilliance, 3–4, 10, 11, 13, 97; cacophony of, 45; changes to, 2, 69–70, 89, fig. *17*, fig. *18*; class and, 6, 20–21, 32–34; as a comfort, 98; contrasting colors, 5, 89, 90–91; Creation and, 2, 3, 12, 75; deceptive quality, 63; decorative colors, 47; devil's tool, 64, 75–76, 87–88, 89; distinct impressions of, 43; divine revelation and, 11; dominant colors in Middle Ages, 61; drab colors, 5, 6, 25, 37, 98; duality of, 10; earthly nature, 66; elusiveness of, 98; expressive value, 44, fig. *4*, fig. *5*, fig. *6*; first color used by God, 84; of fruit, 72; functions, 47; as a gloss, 11; in God's grand design, 6; inherence, 10–11, 12; instability of, 2; intensity and, 11; interchangeability of, 29; language of, 6; light and, 2, 9–10, 13; light colors, 45, 54; linkages with, 11; in literature, 47; liturgical colors, 15; luminosity and, 11; main colors, 15–17; meaning and, 7–8, 44–48; measures of, 2; mixing/blending, 75; as mnemonic device, 47; modern color, 37; negative views of, 1–2; pale colors, 45; passion and, 29–30; perception of, 2–3, 9–10, 14, 44, 87–88; playing with, 47; post-Fall taint, 66–67; primary colors, 18, 85, 97; primitive fascination with, 97; as a reward, 98; in science, 47; secondary colors, 18; as a substance, 10; superstitions about, 12; symbolism (*see* symbol of; symbolism); in television, 36; transience and, 4; truth and, 3; wealth and, 20, 94; wickedness of, 66–67, 71

color preferences: for black, 5; for blond hair, 49; for blue, 4, 5, 44, 49; for brown, 5; children's, 5; for gray, 5; for green, 4, 44; for lavender, 44; for pastels, 36; for purple, 44; for red, 4, 5; for violet, 44; for white, 4, 5; for yellow, 4–5

color reproduction, 8

color schemes: black and blue, 33–34; black and white, 8, 35, 93, 95–97; black-white-gray, 93, 94, 98; green-yellow, 50, 80–81, fig. *12*, fig. *13*; red-white-black, 16–17, 60–61; white and red, 56–58

color symbolism. *See* symbol of; symbolism

colores rhetorici, 1

colorlessness, 65

complexion. *See* skin color

confession manuals, 68

convents: interiors, 67

Corot, Jean-Baptiste-Camille, 3

Coster, Charles de: *Thyl Ulenspiegel,* 93–94

Coter, Colijn de: *Entombment,* fig. 7

Council of Reims (1148), 74

Courtois, Jehan (Sicily Herald): *Blason des couleurs,* 12–13, 26–28, 63, 74, 80; patron, 27

courts (sovereign residences): black and blue fashion, 33–34; color at, 25–26; playacting at, 28–31

Creation: color and, 2, 3, 12, 75; devilish meddling with, 63, 68–69, 70, 75; distortion of, 6; duality of, 78; established order of, 58–59; green linked to, 75, 84; light and, 2; nature and, 40, 78

Crusades, 23, 33

dark colors: acceptance of, 17; blue, 6; brown, 50, 52; clothing and, 34; in depiction of Christ entering Jerusalem, 45; eyebrows, 50, 52; green, 45; in painting, 94–95; plagues and, 34; red, 45; symbolism of, 54

Daubigny, Charles-François, 3

David, 83

De Inventione (Cicero), 1

Decameron (Boccaccio), 35

decoloration, 32–36, 89–98; Bernard of Clairvaux, 3–4, 63, 66, 67; black-and-white color scheme, 8, 35, 95–97; black-white-gray color scheme, 93, 94; blue's popularity, 6, 17–18, fig. *1*; Calvinism and, 7, 36; checkerboard patterns, 74; Christian roots, 6, 63–64; Church's role, 90; clothing and, 32, 67–68, 90; eternal life, 7, 64; Fourth Lateran Council, 67;

13, 66–67, 91–93, fig. *20*; pastels, 95; in 1960s and 1970s, 96
invention: of modern colors, 37; of oil paint, 18, 37–38
Isenheim Altar (Grünewald), fig. *11*
Isidore of Seville, 11
Italy, 9

Jacob and Laban, 74
Jacob Fugger in His Office, fig. *15*
Jans teestye (Boendale), 70
Jerusalem: depiction of Christ's entry into, 45; life as pilgrimage to, 40–41; prediction of destruction of, 78; sack of, 55
jesters, 78, 80
Jesus: Bernard of Clairvaux on, 3–4; body color, 71–72, fig. *7*; Christ the Redeemer, 40; as a decolorer, 65; in depiction of entry into Jerusalem, 45; flagellators of, fig. *9*; Jan van Ruusbroec on, 24; mocker of, fig. *13*; purple and, 24; skin color, 71–72; torturers and executioners of, 72, 73
Jews: Christians distinguished from, 79; Maerlant's view of, 81; red-headedness, 81–82; yellow worn by, 77, 78–79
John the Baptist, 73, fig. *10*
Joinville, Jean de, 33
joy: heavenly joy, 32; personification of, 57; symbol of, 26, 29, 31
Judas, 81, 82, fig. *12*

Kandinsky, Wassily, 85
Karel ende Elegast, 17
knights: clothing, 23; at court, 25; Ferguut, 56; investiture, 31; Lancelot, 79; Mordred, 55–56;

Sagremor, 80; shields, 23; Silvius, 55; tales of, 23, 38, 55–56, 79; Tristan, 80; yellow banner, 78
Koenraad, 75
Koerbecke, Johann: *Christ Before Pilate*, fig. *13*

La Brigue, 72, 92, fig. *12*
Lancelot, 79
landscapes: biblical landscapes, 84; idealization in, 38–39; pleasure from, 42–43
lavender: in depiction of Christ entering Jerusalem, 45; preference for, 44
Le Livre de la Vigne Nostre Seigneur, fig. *17*
Leiden, 20
leisure wear, 93
Levi, 65
Leviathan, 64
Liège, 39
life: as pilgrimage to the heavenly Jerusalem, 40–41; stages of, 15
light: color and, 2, 9–10, 13; Creation and, 2; perception of color and, 9–10; precious stones and, 11
literature (medieval): artisans in, 19–20; Christianizing of old texts, 61; class satire, 19; color in, 47; cross-fertilization of literary traditions, 61; dyers in, 19; function of, 43, 58; ideal feminine beauty in, 51–52, 56–61; ideal life portrayed in, 41; Irish (originally Celtic) texts, 59–61; knightly tales, 23, 38, 55–56, 79; mockeries of marriage, 51; as model of aristocratic behavior, 28; variations on literary convention, 57

pastels (*continued*)
95; preference for, 36; twentieth
century, 93; usage of, 7
Pastor of Hermas (Hermas), 64
peasants: clothing, 33; in *Die buskenblaser,* 69–70; in twelfth-century
France, 98; skin color, 54, 55
perception of color: cultural context's effect on, 44; devil's distor-
tions, 14, 87–88; light and, 9–10;
Van Gogh on, 3; variability of, 2–3
Peter, Saint, 72
Petrarch, 39–40
Philip the Good, 35
physiognomy, 79–80
pigments: *colores rhetorici,* 1; for
purple, 21, 24; for red, 18, 21; for
scarlet, 24; sources, 18, 21; tempera, 37; verbal, 1. *See also* dyes,
dyestuffs
pink: in depiction of Christ entering
Jerusalem, 45; Dutch servants, 94
Pisan, Christine de, 30–31
plague: epidemics affecting fashions
in colors, 34, 35; of grasshopperlike creatures, 9
plays/playacting: actors playing colors, 29–30; black comedy, 19; *Die
Buskenblaser,* 69; and courtly
behavior, 28; early traditions of,
28–30; *Spiel von den sieben Farben*
(Play of the seven colors), 30
pleasance (*locus amoenus*), 39
pleasure: devil and, 43; in nature,
42–43; symbol of, 6, 26
Polyxena, 57
Pompeii, 37
Pont du Gard, 91
Pontius Pilate, 72, fig. 13
Potter, Dirc, 29

precious stones: black backdrop
for, 34; carbuncles, 51, 59; in
church interiors, 3, 91, 92, 93;
colors assigned to, 15; and the
heavenly Jerusalem, 13; light and,
11; on knights' shields, 23; traconite, 97
Priam, King, 57
primary colors: debate about, 18;
love for, 97; status of, 85
primitive peoples: fascination with
color, 97
Protestants: Calvinism, 7, 36;
churches to, 91
Provence, 91
purple: aristocrats, 7, 93; biblical references to, 15; decline of, 93; Jesus
and, 24; lavender, 44; lilac, 94;
pigments for, 21, 24, 93; preference for, 44; symbolism of, 7, 16;
violet, 32, 44, 93; vulgarity, 93

Rabelais, François: on *Blason des
couleurs,* 26–27; on clothing, 27;
Gargantua and Pantagruel, 26
rainbows: colors of, 18, 71; effects
produced by, 89
reason: Christian reason, 80;
dependency on, 41; lack of, 80
recreational vehicles, 65–66
red: apple, 17; biblical references to,
15; blood and, 24; blood-red, 64;
brick red, 45; cheeks, 78; clothing,
67, 83; crimson, 6, 16; dark red,
45; in depiction of Christ entering Jerusalem, 45; a dominant
color, 61; dyestuffs for, 6; elephants and, 12; faces, 50, 52, 82;
God's clothing, 46; madder plant
trade, 18; pigments for, 18, 21;

preference for, 4, 5; prominence of, 16–17; René of Anjou, 32; scarlet, 6, 15, 24, 31; in Spain, 5; symbolism of, 15, 16, 17, 29, 30, 83; undesirability in clothing, 67; as white's opposite, 17

redheadedness, 81–83

Reformation, 36, 92, 93

Reichenau, Abbey of, 45

religious orders: Benedictines, 32; Cistercians, 3, 32, 66, 92; colors associated with, 32, 50, 70; Franciscans, 32, 50, 51, 71, 74–75. *See also* clergy

Renaissance, 38

René of Anjou, King of Sicily, 26, 27, 31–32

Reynard (the Fox), 82

Rinclus, 69

Roman Catholic Church: in decoloration, 90; dilemma, 90; embodiment of, 64; symbol of defense of the Church, 31. *See also* churches

Roman de la Rose, 25–26, 56–57, 71

Roman de Troie, fig. *1,* fig. *2*

romanticism, 93

Rome (ancient), 90

Roovere, Anthonis de, 50–51

Ruusbroec, Jan van, 24, 70

Sagremor (the knight), 80

Saint Mary Magdalene (Master of the Mansi Magdalene), fig. *14*

saints, 71, 73

Salome Receiving the Head of John the Baptist (Lucas van Leyden), fig. *10*

Samson, 83

Satan: deluding human perception,

3; ploys of, 1–2; presence of, 83. *See also* devil; Lucifer

Schwarz, Matthias (*Trachtenbuch*), fig. *15*

secondary colors, 18

self-mutilation, 57

Seuse, Heinrich (Suso), 71–72

Sicily Herald. *See* Courtois, Jehan (Sicily Herald)

Silvius (the knight), 55

Sint Winoksbergen, 83

skin color: aristocrats, 53; children, 11–12, 73; class, 53–54; heroes, 55; Jesus, 71–72; light brown, 54; peasants, 54, 55; red faces, 50, 52, 82; tan, 54, 56; white, 53, 54, 58; women, 52, 53–56

Slovenia, King of, 70

snow: cotton seeming like, 43; in descriptions of feminine beauty, 52, 53, 58, 60, 61; in painted landscapes, 3; cold resulting in white color of, 10;

"Snow White," 17, 56

social class. *See* class

Song of Songs, 38–39

Sorbon, Robert de, 33

sorcerers, 79

Spiegel der sonden, 68, 78

Spiel von den sieben Farben, 30

St. Austremoine in Issoire (Puy-de-Dôme), fig. *20*

St. Laurent, Abbey of, 67

stained-glass windows, 3, 13, 18, 35–36, 46, 73, 89, 91

statuary, 91–92

status. *See* class

Strasbourg Cathedral, 18

stripes, 72–73, 74, 75, fig. *10*

Suger, Abbot of Cluny, 92–93

sunbathing, 54, 56
suntan, 53–56
superstitions about color, 12
swastika: mythical values, 17
symbol of: abnegation, 6; Advent, 16; aggression, 82; alienation, 89; All Souls' Day, 16; angels, 65; Ascension, 15; asceticism, 6; awareness of one's own mortality, 50; betrayal, 79, 82; budding love, 84; celestial robes, 65; charity, 16; chastity, 28; Christmas, 15; cleanliness, 31; constancy, 28; cowardliness, 81; Creation, 75; cuckolds, 86; death, 87; defense of Church, 31; delight, 26; derangement, 80; destruction of the world, 64; determination, 26; devil, 17; devotion, 30; divine revelation, 75; dubious characters, 73; earth, 16, 31, 50, 66; earthly things lacking traces of the divine, 72; Easter, 15; effeminacy, 50; eternity, 64, 75; faith in a happy outcome, 29; faithfulness, 30, 32; fate, 84; feast days, 15–16; feelings, 29, 31–32; fidelity, 28; fire, 16; flight from earthly existence, 64; folly, 50, 80; fools, 80; fortitude, 16; fortune, 84, fig. 15, fig. 16; fulfillment of love, 29; gifts of the Holy Spirit, 16; Good Friday, 16; harmony, 90; heathens, 78; heaven, heavenly joy, 16; hell, 87; Holy Cross, 15; honor, 28; hope, 16, 29, 31, 84; humiliation (voluntary), 50; humility, 6, 29, 50; idiocy, 16; immaculateness, 29; insanity, 50; jealousy, 81; joy, 26, 29, 31; justice, 29; Lent, 16; love, 16, 29; lunacy, 50, 82; luxury, 94; man's state, 54; martyrdom, 16; mendicancy, 32; modesty, 29; mortification, 50; mourning, 34; mourning for a lost love, 29; optimism, 84; paradise, 65; passion, 30; penance, 50; Pentecost, 16; physical world, 64; piety, 16; pleasure, 6, 26; protection, 29; purity, 16, 65, 84; rejoicing, 26; Satan's presence, 83; the sea, 16; servitude, 29; sinlessness, 65; slyness, 82; solemnity, 31; sorrow, 6, 31; steadfastness, 26, 29; stigmatization, 89; strength, 29; style, 90; Sundays after Epiphany, 16; temperance, 29; toil, 34; Trinity, 16; ugliness, 79; ugliness in women, 50; undesirability, 89; untrustworthiness, 79; virtues, 28–29; wantonness, 50; wealth, 94; whores, 66; wickedness, 50, 79–80; wisdom, 29; working days, 16; yearning for immortality, 16
symbolism: of black, 6, 16, 17, 28, 29, 31, 34, 64; of black-sable, 15; of blood-red, 64; of blue, 6, 26, 28, 29, 30, 78, 86–87; of bright colors, 6; of brown, 29, 30, 31, 50; of chess and checker pieces, 17; of clothing, 24–25, 30, 31; of crimson, 16; of dark colors, 54; divine order and, 14–16, 43, 58–59; of fading, 72; of freckles, 54–55; of gold, 28, 64, 78, 80; of gray, 29, 31–32, 34; of green, 16, 29, 75, 80, 84; of green-vermilion, 15; of hyacinth blue, 16; of lilac, 94; of multicoloredness, 72; of purple, 7, 16; Rabelais on, 26–27; of red, 15, 16, 17, 29, 30, 83; of redheadedness, 81–83; of

scarlet, 31; significance of, 44–47; system of, 14; of white, 15, 16, 17, 26, 28, 29, 30, 31, 64, 65, 75, 90; of white flag of surrender, 65; of white-silver, 15; of yellow, 30, 77–78, 79, 80, 81; of yellow-gold, 29

Syria, 55

Tabor, Mount, 43

tan: skin color, 54, 56

television: color in, 36

tempera, 37

Terence, 50, 87

theology/theologians, 5–6, 26, 40, 48, 59

three estates, 32–33

Thyl Ulenspiegel (Coster), 93–94

tournaments, 6, 25

Trachtenbuch (Schwarz), fig. 15

traconite, 97

traffic lights, 81

transformations, 18–20, 69–70. *See also* changeability of color; metamorphoses

Tregement der ghesontheyt, 84–85

Tristan and Isolde, 80

Troy, 17

twentieth century: black-and-white color scheme, 95–96; black-white-gray color scheme, 94; colorless, 97; pastels in, 93

underwear, 65

urban aristocracy, 6

Usnach, 61

Utopia (More), 66

vacations, 7, 65, 96, 98

Various Scenes from the Story of Troy, fig. 2

Veldeke, Hendrik van, 39

Ventoux, Mount, 39

vices: catalogs of virtues and vices, 42, 68; color and, 66

Vier Heemskinderen, 79

Vincent of Beauvais, 10

Virgin Mary. *See* Mary

Virgo Viridissima, 84

viriditas, 84

virtues: catalogs of virtues and vices, 42, 68; dependency on, 41; gifts of the Holy Spirit, 16, 41; interchangeability of, 29; personification, 28; colors symbolic of, 28–29

visual arts, 41, 44, 91

Vogelweide, Walther von der, 17

Voyage d'Outremer (Bertrandon de la Broquière), 43

Walewein, 17, 23

war/warriors: battlefields, 23; brown-skinned warriors, 55; Germanic battle scenes, 83; red-headed warriors, 83; skin color, 55

wealth: colors and, 20; symbol of, 94

weapons, 23–24

white: biblical references to, 15; cold and, 10; a dominant color, 61; dual nature, 10; God and, 68; God's clothing, 46; heat and, 10; Leviathan's head, 64; as a non-color, 6, 35, 64–65; opposites, 17; preference for, 4, 5; prominence of, 16–17; Rabelais on, 27; recreational vehicles, 65–66; René of Anjou, 31, 32; skin color, 53, 54, 58; in stained glass, 35–36; symbolism of, 15, 16, 17, 26, 28, 29, 30, 31, 64, 65, 66, 75, 90; timelessness, 97;

white (*continued*)
     underwear, 65; vehicles, 65–66;
     women and, 68
white-silver: symbolism of, 15
Whore of Babylon, 83
whores: Blue Beguines, 86; Blue Bet,
     86; redheadedness, 82; color sym-
     bolic of, 66; yellow badges, 79
William of Auvergne, 84
William of Lübeck, 79
witches, 79, 87
women, 49–61; adulterous women,
     79, 82; baby's color, 11–12, 73;
     Bernard of Clairvaux on, 68;
     black in, 51; blondes, 49–50, 52;
     brown in, 51; in Celtic texts,
     59–61; children of miscegenation,
     73; clothing, 6, 25; color combina-
     tions, 75; conception during
     menstruation, 82; Deirdre, 61;
     Ecclesia, 64; Etain, 59–61; eye-
     brows, 50, 52; eyes, 49–50; facial
     beauty, 51–52, 56–58; Galiene, 56;
     hair color, 49–50, 52, 53; head-
     scarves, 68; ideal beauty, 50–53,
     59–61; instrument of ruin, 4;
     makeup, 68–70; modesty of, 29,
     68; Molhem on, 69; painting

themselves, 4, 69; personification
     of virtue, 28; playacting, 28;
     Polyxena, 57; skin color, 52, 53–56;
     ugliness in, 50; white and red
     color scheme, 56–58; white for,
     68; whores, 66, 79, 82, 86
workers, 20–21
Wotan, 83
Württemberg, Hendrik van,
     77–78

yellow: aversion to, 49; clothing, 67,
     78; in depiction of Christ enter-
     ing Jerusalem, 45; disparagement
     of, 77–80; eyes, 78; gradations of,
     83; headscarves, 68; idiomatic
     expressions with, 81; Jews, 77,
     78–79; knight's banner, 78; light
     yellow, 45; Muslims, 77, 79; pale
     yellow, 45; physiognomy and, 79;
     positive manifestation, 49; prefer-
     ence for, 4–5; saffron yellow, 4, 68,
     79; in stained glass, 35–36; sun-
     light, 49; symbolism of, 30, 77–78,
     79, 80, 81; traffic lights, 81; unde-
     sirability in clothing, 67; yellow
     badges, 78–79; yellow-gold, 29;
     yellowish-green, 16–17